About the Author

Dr. **Nandita Babu** is currently a Reader in Department of Psychology at University of Delhi. She is pursuing research and teaching in various areas such as early childhood development, development of theory of mind and language in children, culture and child development and developmental psychopathology. She was awarded with Common Wealth Scholarship in 1985 for pursuing Doctorate degree at the University of Toronto, Canada while she was working as a lecturer at Utkal University, Bhubaneswar. As a faculty at Utkal University (1982-2002), she was actively involved in extension works of early childhood teacher training programmes, child rearing practices parent training programmes organized by SCERT and UNICEF. She is also associated with organizations like NCERT, DIPR and INCLEN. She has published numerous papers on cognitive and language development in children in various journals of repute and written chapters in book's as well.

DEVELOPMENT OF THEORY OF MIND AND MENTAL STATE LANGUAGE IN CHILDREN

Dr.(Mrs.) Nandita Babu

Department of Psychology

University of Delhi

CONCEPT PUBLISHING COMPANY, NEW DELHI-110059

Cataloging in Publication Data—DK
Courtesy: D.K. Agencies (P) Ltd. <docinfo@dkagencies.com>

Babu, Nandita.
Development of theory of mind and mental state language in children / Nandita Babu.
p. cm.
Study conducted at rural and semi-urban areas around Cuttack and Khurda districts of Orissa, India.
Includes bibliographical references (p.).
Includes index.
ISBN 13: 9788180695155
ISBN 10: 8180695158

1. Oriya language—Acquisition. 2. Children—India—Orissa—Language. 3. Philosophy of mind in children—India—Orissa. I. Title.

DDC 155.413 095 413 3 22

ISBN-13: 978-81-8069-515-5
ISBN-10: 81-8069-515-8

First Published 2009

Published and Printed by
Ashok Kumar Mittal
Concept Publishing Company
A/15-16, Commercial Block, Mohan Garden
New Delhi-110059 (India)

Phones : 25351460, 25351794
Fax : 091-11-25357109
Email : publishing@conceptpub.com
Website : www.conceptpub.com

Foreword

Children's mind is a fascinating empire. Over the ages, countless number of explorer's have sought to discover this empire, to know, to understand, to revel at the marvels of a human mind in the making. Every time some discovery is accomplished, it becomes evident that a lot more remains; the mystery multiplies endlessly.

Here is yet another exploration, but one with some difference in purpose, some uniqueness in methods and some prolonged pursuit towards discovery, if not an exact discovery, *per se*. How do children come to know what is there in the minds: of their own and of others? What and how do they understand a variety of shades of mental states? This endeavour is based on an assumption that not only do children develop knowledge and understanding of mental states, they also come to acquire a theory of mind, a theory in deeper sense—systematic, coherent, explanatory and predictive. Children are credited with critical awareness and understanding of a reality at a different plane, the reality that is not a direct result of the physical and objective world but one that is created in the mind. In the processes children come to a whole set of mental state descriptor words such as know, think, believe, guess, pretend, hope, desire, etc. with finer discriminations. This rising from one level of reality to another, from the physical to the phenomenological, is yet another very wonderful facet of the vast unexplored, under explored empire of children's mind. As Dr. Nandita Babu rightly observes, the movement from one level to the other in children's understanding of mental states and their metarepresentational system is, at least partly, an outcome of a very complex interplay of processes of cognition and the processes of language and communication. At one level, the latter evidently emerges out of the former, but, at another level, the cognitive processes barely remain unaffected by growing skills with language. At the same time, Dr. Babu seeks to show that the agency for this complex emergence of a Theory of Mind does not lie in the child alone, the socio-cultural processes have significant inputs into this process. Like mind, theory of mind is also jointly constructed.

Human learning is not just an externally corrected but an internally self-corrective process. Complex learning is not quite possible without self-regulation and monitoring. Language acquisition of children is a gradual process in which children show remarkable ability to reflect and improve upon their utterances. Correction of own speech (and sometimes of others, too) is quite common in children. Similar processes of monitoring are also in evidence in respect of various other cognitive activities that children engage in. It seems these mechanisms of internal monitoring and correction, without which language and other complex skills would be hard to acquire, gradually evolve to act as control processes underlying adult level cognition. These have generally been characterized as metacognitive processes with specific manifestation such as metalinguistic ability, metamemory and so on. As Dr. Babu shows in this monograph, there is a close relationship between development of linguistic, metalinguistic and metacognitive abilities and development of children's theory of mind. It can be argued that theory of mind as well as metacognitive controls have a common origin in children's ability to self-reflect, to monitor and to cognize other's mental processes. It is also true that once the metacognitive processes are developed, children's conceptualization of reality goes to a different plane of being a constructed phenomenon.

This monograph by Dr. Babu deals effectively with several questions that may be raised in respect of development of a theory of mind. A very crucial issue which has cross-linguistic and cross-cultural relevance is whether certain aspects of metarepresentational skills are related to existence of metarepresentational language to which a child is exposed. While no language is inadequate to express metarepresentational thought or different mental states, it is possible that the nature of metarepresentational usages and their frequencies in routine social interactions may vary from one language to another depending upon specific cultural requirements and communicative priorities. In this monograph the author explores patterns of Oriya language use in a variety of contexts to analyse the existence of metarepresentational language. She gives an analysis and classification of different types of Oriya metarepresentational terms. But, at the same time, she rightly observes, mental state words do not necessarily indicate metarepresentational ability. In other words, mere use of words cannot be taken as sufficient evidence for existence of mental state understanding. Dr. Babu's analysis points to two clear possibilities. One, metarepresentational skills are universal across different languages and cultures. Two, there may be language and culture-specific manifestations of the pattern of development of theory of mind.

Dr. Babu's explorations into the theory of mind goes into analysis of the nature of acquisition of metarepresentational words and understanding of mental states. She speaks of children's acquisition occurring in two phases. The early phase is characterized by use and basic understanding of metarepresentational words and the later phase by elaboration of the words and understanding acquired during the earlier phase. In other words, children seem to be moving from a routine use of mental state words prevalent in their linguistic input and contextual understanding of the same in cognitively less demanding situations to more cognitive and abstract use and understanding. Similar distinctions between levels of mental processes are quite frequent in psychological literature dealing with aspects of cognition and, in fact, they are quite useful in explaining several anomalies in studies of human development.

Apart from looking at the development of children's theory of mind, Dr. Babu looks at the role of socio-cultural variables in such development. Her attempts at relating parental literacy and other socio-cultural conditions to use and understanding of mental state descriptors are quite interesting. That parent's input language seems to be sensitive to the level of children's development is very significant. Parents are found to be using metarepresentational language more often with older than with younger children. This is significant in understanding the nature of joint socio-cultural construal of mind as well as theory of mind.

On the whole, this monograph is a good exploration into children's metarepresentational processes and their theory on mind. The author raises some very vital questions and provides answers to them. To me, understanding of the processes of development of theory of mind is also significant from a different contemporary perspective. There is a lot of interest in the current psychological literature on implicit theories of psychological processes and phenomena. Such implicit theories are popular constructions that reside in the minds of lay persons (and even psychologists). Implicit theories are constructed with the usual theories in psychology and other behavioural sciences—explicit theories invented by researchers to explain data regarding behaviour and experience. People hold beliefs about psychological processes; at one level each person acts (and reacts) like a psychologist operating on the basis of his/her belief about how aspects of human mind function. These implicit theories do, in fact, provide the basis for people to assess others as well as themselves. Implicit theories are internally constructed and socio-culturally shared systems. With increasing emphasis on indigenous perspectives in psychological theories across cultures, discovery of implicit theories in cultures and sub-cultures has gained significance. It seems, the processes of construction of implicit theories can be traced to the early development of children's theory of mind. Growing understanding of mental states and use of language to describe own and other's mental states are perhaps the beginning of construction of implicit theories, which, of course, are much broader in scope. It would be interesting to understand how children make this transition from a theory of mind to many implicit theories of a variety of psychological processes such as intelligence, creativity, personality and so on. It is quite evident that language and metalanguage plays a crucial role in construction of a theory of mind as well as in implicit theorization. Dr. Babu's emphasis on linguistic as well as metalinguistic processes and her explorations and methodology show how the processes of such theory formation can be systematically deconstructed. Her work paves the way for a critical understanding of construction of implicit theories providing significant leads which need to be followed.

This monograph is a significant attempt and has ingredients of making an impact. It touches upon a very complex aspect of children's mind, which at one level is obvious; at another enigmatic. The work is one more good attempt at exploring the fascinating empire of children's mind. It cannot but arouse interest among all students of human mind. I commend the book and thank Dr. Nandita Babu, the author for a chance to preview its contents.

Ajit K. Mohanty
Professor of Psychology
ZHCSE, JNU

Preface

This book primarily focuses upon the relationship between the development of mental state language and theory of mind. Mental state language is considered to be expressions which we use to talk about mind. For example, when one could distinctly use the statements "I know he is a film star" and "I guess he is a film star", it is obvious that he understands the difference between the two underlying mental state of "knowing" and "guessing". The language that is used to talk about mind falls within the ever controversial discussion of the relationship between language and thought. Traditionally language and thought relationship is discussed within two different perspectives on cognitive development. The Piagetian perspective in which language depends on thought and the Vygotskian perspective in which thought depends on language. In accordance with the former view, the acquisition of mental state vocabulary reflects children's acquisition of mental state reasoning or theory of mind. On the contrary in accordance with the later view, mental state language use in adult-child conversation in their cultural context facilitates their acquisition of a theory of mind. There is research evidence in support of both these perspectives in the literature. Keeping in view the prevailing debate on the relationship between mental state language and theory of mind a number of research questions are addressed in the present book. Some of these questions are:

- Does the acquisition of mental state language is a general acquisition irrespective of the language spoken by the child or is it language specific ? In other words are all languages equally equipped with mental state expressions?
- Does the use of mental state language is context dependent? Or Is there any variation in use of such language from

formal to informal discourse, or from written to oral discourse?

- Does the use of mental state language vary as a function of literacy level of the speaker?

Till date the available literature provides research data on American-European languages. Research on native speakers of English language indicates that around 3 to 4 years children start to talk about mental states using mental state language. In the present book an attempt was made to look at some of the issues discussed above with the help of research findings obtained in a study undertaken by the author in Oriya language. The various dimensions of the relationship between development of mental state vocabulary and children's theory of mind is examined in the different chapters of the book. The first two chapters primarily focus upon the theoretical exposition of the newly evolving field of research: theory of mind (ToM) and mental state language. The second part of the book deals with 4 major research issues pertaining to development of a theory of mind and mental state language. Each research issue is supported by research data. First of all, an attempt was made to analyse Oriya language (a regional language in India) to find out the existence of mental state language in it. It is important, because prior to investigating the development of mental state language it was required to know the extent of use of such language by the native speaker of Oriya or any other language in question. Chapter 3 deals with such an analysis of Oriya language. The second issue is developemnt of metarepresentational language. The focus of the book is the period from 2 years to 12 years of age, and the 4th and 5th chapters consider developmental changes across this age range. The 4th chapter deals with early acquisition of metarepresentational words whereas the 5th chapter deals with elaboration of such words in the higher age groups. The third issue dealt with in this book is the role of socio-cultural variables on acquisition of metarepresentational words. It is covered in the 3rd and 4th chapter while discussing the development of mental state words. The last issue is the cognitive and academic implications of acquiring a set of mental state words. This is also discussed in the 3rd and 4th chapter along with research evidences. An attempt was made to assess whether acquisition of mental state words is fundamental to children's readiness for school and at a later age whether further elaboration of such words are necessary for their academic achievement.

Nandita Babu

Acknowledgements

I wish to express my gratitude to ERIC, NCERT for the financial grant for the research reported in this book. I am deeply indebted to Prof. D.P. Pattnaik, Director (Retd.), Central Insitute of Indian Languages, Mysore, India, for his advice during the conduction of the research and Prof. Ajit Kumar Mohanty, ZHSCE, JNU, for his comments and suggestions during preparation of the manuscript. I would also like to thank Subhasmita Panda and Nidhi Goel for their help during the preparation of manuscript. Last but not least, I wish to thank Concept Publishing Company for publishing this book.

Nandita Babu

Contents

List of Tables and Figures

FIGURES

Chapter-1

Developing a Theory of Mind

Mental states like beliefs and desire are representations that moderate our activity in the world. They provide us with a psychological relationship to reality. Imagine a scene cited by Astington (1993): A man comes home from the store with a bag of apples, which he puts into the refrigerator before he goes out to the backyard. The wife comes into the kitchen looking for something to eat. She sees the apples in the refrigerator, takes one and bites into it. Finding it too cold she moves the apples to the cupboard. Later the man returns to the kitchen. "I am hungry", he says, "I'll have an apple". We are not surprised that he looks in the refrigerator, nor are we surprised when he finds no apples there. Our lack of surprise demonstrates some fundamental aspects of our commonsense understanding of mental representation. First, we believe there is a real world out there, which include real things like apples, the refrigerators. These things exist independent of our thoughts about them. Second, we believe we do have thoughts about these things and sometimes those thoughts don't reflect the ways things really are in the world. We act not on the basis of the way things really are, but on the basis of the way we think they are:

> *You can also try this activity with a 3 year and a 5 year old and observe how they respond.*
> *Show a gems (candies) box to a 5 year old and ask what she thinks is inside the box, she would reply "gems" (in reality there are pencils in that box). Ask her to open it, when she opens it she will be surprised by finding pencils in it. When asked what would another child who has not seen inside the box, would think is in the box, the child would very comfortably*

> *reply "Gems of Course!". To your surprise a 3 year old would reply in the same way to the first question but not to the second question. Most likely she would reply "pencils" when asked the second question. Take another instance. Show two boxes to a 3 year old, one is a gems box with pencils in it and the other is a pencil box with gems in it. Allow her to see the contents as well. Later on if you ask her, which box would another child, who has not seen the contents of the box, open to get some gems, the 3 year old would most likely say, the "pencil box". If asked "why would the other child open this box," The 3 year old would say "because there are gems in it" or "because he wants to eat some".*

The 3 year old in the first and second example are unable to understand the distinction between mind and reality. They consider mind to be identical with reality, and other's mind to be same as their mind, whereas the 5 year old's explanation clearly indicates that she distinguishes between what she thinks, what the other thinks and what the reality is. She knows that her mental representation matches with reality but not that of the other. The 5 year old understands that while she knows what is in the gems box, the other does not have this knowledge and rather holds a false belief. We can characterise the 5 year old's understanding by saying that the 5 year old understands that mind consists of such states as knowledge, belief, desire, emotions, which one can refer to while explaining ones own as well as others behaviour. Here the child behaves just like a psychologist. Psychologists want to know why people do what they do and they explain by referring to their theoretical positions like "she is reinforced to open the box, or her brain is not fully developed", etc. However, in everyday conversation people explain behaviour by saying, "She wanted to eat some chocolate", "She thinks there are gems in the box", "She was sad when she did not get any" etc. This is our commonsense psychology or folk psychology. If you compare the responses of the 5 year old and the 3 year old child cited in the beginning you would agree that the 5 year old has a folk psychological concept or explains behaviour by refering to mind whereas the 3 years old are yet to acquire any folk psychological or everyday psychological concepts. Everyday psychology is often called belief-desire psychology. But the words "belief" and "desire" don't have their common conversational meanings, where beliefs are things taken as faith, such as religious convictions, and desire is lust or longing for something. Beliefs and desires in this context simply refer to mental states of taking something as true or simply wanting. In order to understand, explain and predict others behaviour we attribute mental states such as beliefs, intentions, desires etc. These are all states of mind. These states of mind originate in the brain, in neural activity, but the mind is not the brain, it is the sum of these mental states or mental representations. Folk psychology simply assumes that beliefs and desires exist. It assumes that people have minds that are the sum of their beliefs, desires, emotions and intentions.

Thus during early childhood children begin to distinguish between the world and mental representation of the world. Children grow up to recognise themselves and others as "things" (entities) which think, believe, doubt, wonder, imagine, pretend, etc. It is not just another addition of a piece of knowledge to their existing knowledge base; rather it is a fundamental alteration in their orientation towards their knowledge of own as well as others. Developmental psychologists termed it as "theory of mind" (ToM). Why is this acquisition termed as a "theory of mind"? As suggested by Wellman (1988), a theory consists of a referential domain, that is, the set of events to be explained and predicted, and a set of rules for using the theoretical concepts to explain and predict events in the referential domain. In the case of a theory of mind, the events to be explained and predicted are talk and action; and the theoretical concepts are beliefs, desires, intentions, etc. These theoretical concepts represent states that are not directly observable but can be inferred from overt action and talk. Children's acquisition of a theory of mind is also marked by their acquisition of language referring to mental states or mental representation (Astington, Harris & Olson, 1988).

It should be noted here that a theory of mind goes beyond the possession of these concepts. As these concepts represent such states as beliefs, desires, and intentions, they constitute representations of representations and therefore, constitute metarepresentational system or recursive thought. In this book mental representation is considered as a mental state: thought, want, belief, intention and so on. Awareness of such representations in self and others is referred to as metarepresentation.

The term theory of mind was first used, in this context, by Premack and Woodruff (1978) in their research on chimpanzees. They claimed that chimpanzees can predict human actions. They showed chimpanzee videotapes in which a human actor in an animal cage faced problems trying to reach a bunch of bananas outside the cage. At the end, they showed the animal two photographs: one giving a solution to the problem, for example, the actor reaching out of the cage with a stick and the other providing no solutions whatsoever. They found that the chimpanzee could readily choose the picture of the solution and not the other picture, which did not reflect any solution. On the basis of this finding, Premack and Woodruff (1978, p. 515) concluded that chimpanzees have a theory of mind. "*In saying that an individual has a theory of mind, we mean that the individual imputes mental states to himself and to others.... A system of inferences of this kind is properly viewed as a theory, first because such states are not directly observable and second because the system can be used to make predictions, specifically, about the behaviour of other organisms... purpose or intention is the state we impute most widely.*"

Later, Wimmer and Perner (1983) developed an experimental paradigm to study children's understanding of others' mind. Since then, children's development of a theory of mind has been the focus of much research in the field of developmental psychology.

Research on theory of mind, sometimes also referred to as mentalizing, mind reading, folk psychology or belief-desire psychology in children began in the early 1980s and today interest in young children's understanding of their own and other's mental lives has become one of the most active and fastest growing areas of research in developmental psychology. Theory of mind has been viewed as the foundation of our appreciation of literature, opera, drama and film. It animates our humour and helps us make sense of the complex patterns of social relationships that surrounds us, including acts of deception.

Before going into details of children's acquisition of a theory of mind, a discussion on the philosopher's and the psychologist's view of the importance of intentionality to explain and predict human action seems to be in order.

Dennett (1987) described three different stances or ways in which we can explain and predict what someone or something does. First, the physical stance predicts and explains the behaviours of a machine by taking its mechanical parts into consideration. For example, the lever, the wheels, and cogs of an alarm clock are set in a particular way to give the correct time. But this stance fails to explain behaviour when there are differences in the physical structure of the machine. Second, the functional stance predicts and explains behaviour by referring to the design of a machine. By taking this stance, it can be said that they behave the way they are designed to behave. This stance is also inadequate to explain human behaviour. Third, the intentional stance predicts and explains behaviour of animals or persons, but certainly not of objects or machines (except of an intelligent computer) by referring to intentional states (Brentano, 1960) such as one's belief, desires and intentions. Dennett's intentional stance is the conceptual basis of a theory of mind or commonsense psychology or folk psychology. Here, "intentional" is used as a technical philosophical term and not in the ordinary sense meaning "deliberate" or "on purpose". This intentionality has more recently and colloquially been referred to as "aboutness". Intentional or mental states are always about something, objects and events in the world or perhaps non-existent things (Astington, 1993). Dennett has suggested that one can differentiate between different levels of intentionality. In the zero-order level, i.e., in the absence of intentionality, the behaviour of the system can be explained by the physical or design stance. In the first order level, the systems behaviour can be explained by referring to its beliefs and desires. However, the system has no beliefs about others' beliefs. The second order intentional system is a recursive system. It has beliefs about its own and others beliefs. These beliefs and desires are mental representations providing a psychological link with the real world.

The characterisation of these states in terms of "intentionality" can be traced back to Brentano (1960). Recent exponents of intentionality theory are Fodor (1987), Pylyshyn (1978), and Searle (1983) all of whom adopted a realist stance to intentional states as the base for human behaviour. Searle, for example, stated, "Intentionality is so to speak a ground floor property of the mind" (1984, p. 26).

Olson (1988) opined that intentional states consist not only of representations of the world, but also of "attitudes" to those representations; consequently, behaviour is a function not just of the propositional content ("that today is Saturday") but also of the holder's attitude to that content, that it is believed, desired or doubted. According to Olson, before the acquisition of language, children's behaviour may be characterised in non-intentionalist terms. Once they acquire a language for stating propositions, their behaviours may be characterised in intentional terms, even if these intentional states are not subject to awareness or manipulation by their holders. Finally, with conscious awareness of intentional states, they become metarepresentational. Olson suggested three different stages in the development of intentionality. In the first stage, before the acquisition of language, behaviour may be characterised by habits (If A do B) or expectancies (If A then B). A theorist may represent such habits and expectancies in terms of propositions, but these are not represented by the child in the form of propositions. In the second stage, the child becomes intentional with the acquisition of language. For example, if the child asks for X, he desires X, if he says that P, he thinks that P. But the child does not yet think of these states as representational states. Finally, in the third stage, children acquire a theory of mind that permits them to think of their own and others' talk and action in terms of mental states. The origin of beliefs and other intentional states may be tied to the acquisition of language. As discussed earlier, the social processes, which make cognition and language possible, are facilitated by the child's understanding of intentionality. For Olson, "the beginning of belief and the beginning of an awareness of those beliefs are both tied to the acquisition of language. The former depends upon the acquisition of a language for formulating and expressing propositions, the latter depends on the acquisition of a metalanguage for talking about those propositions" (Olson, 1988, p. 423).

Major Theoretical Accounts

The mechanisms underlying the development of a concept mind or mental representation are the subject of considerable debate. The questions researchers ponder about are: What kinds of knowledge underlie these abilities? and how can we explain the origin of and changes in children's understanding of mind?

One of the most prominent recent views sees acquisition of the concept of mind as development of a theory and as discussed earlier the general field has come to be known as children's theories of mind. Several other psychologists and philosophers have taken different perspective to the development of the concept of mind in children. In the following section some of these explanations are discussed.

Theory Theory

Theory theorists argue that older children and adult's knowledge of the mind consists of a theory and that development in theory of mind is essentially one of hypothesis testing. These arguments are part of a more general tendency to think of cognitive development in terms of theory formation (Carey, 1985, 1988; Gopnik, 1988; Karmiloff-Smith, 1988). Development of a theory does not mean an actual scientific theory, but more of an informal theory, much in the same way as we can be said to hold informal theories about other domains such as physics. In our everyday conception of physics we do not attempt to provide a complete scientific account of why, for example when we kick a ball, it rolls away from us. Instead we simply understand that the impact of a moving object (our foot) upon a stationary one (the ball) sets the latter in motion.

The theory theorists thus argue that we make use of an informal theory, or a conceptual framework, that fits several criteria. First, the theoretical entities (e.g. beliefs, desires, and intentions) are far removed from reality. Second, these entities are coherent and interrelated. In order to explain one's action we need to understand how beliefs, desires and intentions interconnect to produce a particular intention to act. Third, there is complex law, like interrelationship between these entities. Theories allow one to generalize, to predict and to explain. They have complicated relation to evidence. On the one hand they may serve to insulate the knower from counter evidence at least for a while and may lead them to reinterpret or ignore it. On the other hand, theories eventually change when faced with counter examples to their predictions. Finally, theories are domain specific: one may have a highly advanced theory in one area of knowledge and a relatively simple one in others. The important point to state over here is that, the mechanism of development according to this view is internal to the theory formation process itself. Theory development is the result of both internal structural factors within the theory, a drive for simplicity, for example, and external factors such as accumulation of confirming or disconfirming evidence.

Researchers with the theory theory perspective have identified several milestones in children's acquisition of an adult theory of mind. Gopnik and Slaughter (1991) suggested three-step model of development. Step 1: Understanding of pretence, perception and imagination. These states according to Gopnik and Slaughter are non-representational and therefore, are the easiest. Step 2: Understanding of desire and intention. These states are thought to be of intermediate difficulty as they are representational states with conditions of satisfaction rather than truth conditions. Finally, Step 3: understanding of belief and desire. These states are the most difficult because they are representational states with truth conditions.

Bartsch and Wellman (1995) suggested a three-step developmental sequence of children's development towards an adult ToM . They argue that children go through at least two fundamental theory shifts before they reach a fully developed belief-desire psychology. First, around the age of two, children acquire a simple desire psychology. This psychology includes an elementary conception not only of simple desires, but also of simple emotions and simple perceptual experience or attention. The conception is elementary in the sense that although mentalistic, it is non-representational rather than representational. That is the child understands that other people are subjectively connected to things in the sense of having the inner experience of wanting, fearing, and seeing them etc., but the child does not yet understand that people mentally represent these things. Second, around age three, children begin to talk about beliefs and thoughts as well as desires, and they seem to understand that beliefs are mental representations that are not always consistent with reality and other people do not always hold the same belief as their own. However, at this stage children continue to explain their own, as well as others action in terms of desires rather than beliefs. Bartsch and Wellman (1995) termed this stage as desire-belief psychology. Finally, at about age four, children begin to understand that what people think and believe as well as what they desire, will have an affect on how they behave. That is, they acquire an adult belief-desire psychology, an understanding that beliefs and desires together determine behaviour.

Theory theorists argue that experience helps in shaping children's ToM development. They believe that experience provides information to young children and eventually help them revise and improve their theory. For example, the desire psychologist will gradually become the belief psychologist by repeatedly experiencing situations where people behave according to their beliefs as well as desires (Flavell, 1988). Essentially, according to this view, the process of development is one of hypothesis testing.

Modularity Theory

Other theorists (Baron-Cohen, 1995; Fodor, 1992; Leslie, 1994; Leslie, Friedman & German, 2004; Mitchell, 1994) have different views about what is acquired in ToM development and how. Almost everybody agrees that theory of mind development is dependent upon the biological maturation of genetically based neurocognitive structures, or modules, of the brain. Leslie (1994) and Leslie *et al.* (2004), for example, postulates the acquisition of ToM through neurological maturation of a succession of domain-specific and modular mechanisms for dealing with agents *versus* non-agent objects. A mechanism called Theory of Body (ToBY) develops early in the first year. It allows the baby to recognize, among other things, that agents have an internal source of energy that permits them to move on their own (Flavell, 1999).The next two mechanisms called Theory of Mind Mechanisms (ToMM) deals with the intentionality of agents rather than with their mechanical properties. ToMM1, which develops later in the first year, allows the infant to understand that people and other agents perceive the environment and pursue different goals. ToMM2 begins to develop during the second year of life. This mechanism allows children to represent agents as holding attitudes towards the truth of propositions— propositional attitudes similar to the argument of Olson cited earlier. Propositional attitudes are mental states such as pretending that, believing that, imagining that, desiring that, thinking that, etc. In addition to having the ToMM's children must, according to Leslie, also be equipped with a selection procedure (SP). It is the SP that makes it possible for children to perform executive functions such as inhibiting a pre-potent response on the false-belief task, i.e. not to blurt out the salient real location of the chocolate in the Maxi task when asked about the other person's belief about its content.

Mental Simulation Theory

Theorists in this group argue that children develop concept of mind through experience and not through maturation or theory building. Some in this group say that children's early understanding is intuitive, rather than theoretical (e.g. Johnson, 1988). What the child understands is her own phenomenal experience. Through introspection, she becomes aware of her own desires, beliefs and feelings and then uses this awareness in understanding others. Harris (1991) develops this idea in some detail. He argues that the child who, for example, tells you where the other persons would search for the chocolate in the false belief task, is not making any theoretical prediction, but is engaging in mental simulation.

The simulation account has a strong backup in the philosophical tradition about the nature of psychological knowledge. On this view, which conventionally has been identified with Descartes, introspective, first person psychological knowledge is the foundation of all sorts of knowledge. This view is spelt out in the philosophical literature of Goldman (1989) and Gordon (1986). The implication of this position for development of theory of mind is that: children are introspectively aware of their own mental states and can use this awareness to infer the mental states of other people through a kind of role-taking or simulation process. It should be noted here that there are some contradictory evidence to the simulation perspective. Nisbet and Ross (1980) evidenced adult's inaccurate reporting of their own motivations and desires. In theory of mind research also it was observed that children are no better at reporting their own immediate past mental states than they are at attributing similar mental states to others (Gopnik and Slaughter, 1991).

The Enculturation Hypothesis

A radically different view suggests that theory of mind develops to help us in regulating our interaction with others and is primarily the result of socialization or enculturation. According to this view theory of mind is what Wittgenstein would call a 'form of life' a set of social and cultural practices and conventions. Bruner (1989, 1990) viewed that children's developing understanding of mind is dependent on their growing up in a particular linguistic and cultural environment. Dunn (1988) provides detailed observations of young children's family life that illuminates this view. Although th theory theory view and the enculturation view share the idea that children develop a concept of mind, their accounts of the mechanism of development are very different. Theories always develop with reference to the outside world, the truth whereas cultural practices are self-constitutive and are either right or wrong. If enculturation hypothesis were correct then wide variations in cultural specific explanations and predictions of behaviours would be observed.

Chapter-2

Theory of Mind and Mental State Language

Human interaction is essentially an interaction of minds, of mental states. People have beliefs about others, desire to make others believe something; believe that others intend to do something and so on. However, this social interaction does not proceed directly *via* the interaction of mental states, it proceeds indirectly by way of communication which frequently involves language. In cognitive and educational psychology we frequently come across terms like metacognitive, metamemory, metalinguistic. These terms refer to processes of a second order. Metacognitive processes operate as cognitive processes, thus implying some awareness on one's own cognition. Metalinguistic refers to one's awareness of language; metalinguistic terms are used to talk about language. Metarepresentation terms are a general set of terms used to talk about representation in thought and in language. And metarepresentational ability otherwise known as theory of mind (ToM) is one's reflection on one's own and other's representations or mental states.

The relationship between language and thought is a complex and problematic one. When a person uses a mental state word to make a statement or pose a question about some mental state or process, this necessarily constitutes awareness of knowledge about mental state or process. Thus, any literal use of a mental state word by definition, involves an act of metacognition on the part of the speaker. One of the purposes for investigating the use of mental state words is their relationship with metacognition and metarepresentation, i.e. their role in a person's knowledge about, or awareness of mental states and processes.

The fact that children by 4 years of age have become language using creatures when they begin to form metarepresentations, suggest that language or a more general symbolic capacity may be an important element in the development of this understanding. The fact, that children are acquiring a mentalistic vocabulary about this time, suggests that these vocabularies play an important role. Mental state words are obviously crucial for communicating about mental states to others, so it is likely enough that they play a role in thinking about mental states as well. The extent, to which language in general and such distinctive predicates (mental state words) in particular, are relevant to the achievement of a theory of mind, remains an important but unresolved issue.

Hood and Bloom (1979) reported that in their everyday conversations, even 2 year olds often attempt to explain why people do things. Similarly, Dunn, Bretherton, and Munn (1987) found that by 2 years of age, a majority of children referred to a range of internal states in themselves and others, and discussed the cause of such states in a variety of everyday contexts. People's actions and reactions figure substantially in young children's talk. The period between 18 months and 5 years of age is the time during which children's theory of mind develops and it is also the major period of language development (Gopnik, 1988). Further, it is well established that children with autism, who generally fail theory of mind tasks, are delayed in their language achievements and have different patterns of linguistic performance from normal children (Tager-Flusberg, 1993).

A few recent experimental studies have found a strong correlation between language and theory of mind measures.

Bryant and Furrow (1999) have found that performance on the theory of mind tasks correlates with performance on a test of children's understanding of the words think and know. Bartsch and Wellman (1995) have published a comprehensive study of the naturalistic use of belief and desire terms and related the findings to experimental work in theory of mind development. Some research on story comprehension suggests that younger children are especially dependent on mental state concepts. Gruencich and Trabasso (1979) reviewed a number of experimental studies which suggest that mental state words are important for children's acquisition and organisation of the associated mental concepts. Satpathy (1993) in a study found a strong correlation between understanding of reality-belief distinction and children's use of metarepresentational words. As children's use of metarepresentational terms increased, their ability to distinguish the reality-belief concepts and understanding of sources of knowledge increased.

Now, what aspects of language are involved in the relation between language and theory of mind? Astington Jenkins (1995) pointed out: Obviously pragmatics is. Language use is premised on a theory of mind : "without a theory of mind, one cannot participate in a conversation" (de Gelder, 1987). Indeed, some time ago Bretherton and her colleagues argued that 1 and 2 year old's communicative abilities imply that even very young children have a theory of mind (Bretherton, 1991). There is also a relation between language and theory of mind at the syntactic level. During the preschool years children achieve mastery of the basic syntactic forms of their language, including object complements needed to refer to the propositional content of a mental state (e.g., 'He "thinks" the chocolate is in the cupboard'—object complement within inverted commas). Other researchers (de Villiers, 1995, Tager-Flusberg, 1995) demonstrated the relations that exist between theory of mind tasks and syntactic tasks, using complement-taking verbs. Astington and Jenkins (1995) in a longitudinal study have found that the children whose language was better developed were more likely to develop their theory of mind skills. They used the Test of Early Language Development (Hresko, Reid Hammill, 1981). In the same study they got the evidence of mutual boosting between theory of mind and use of mental verbs. Children, according to them use cognitive verbs before they can perform successfully on theory of mind tasks.

Researches in the area of development of a theory of mind and development of language suggest a strong correlation between language ability and theory of mind measures (Astington & Baird,

2005). The period between 18 months and 5 years of age is the time during which children's theory of mind develops and it is also the major period of acquisition of mental state terms such as think, know, believe, etc. Most of these studies (Astington & Jenkins, 1999; de Villers & de Villers, 2000; Watson, Painter & Bornstein, 2002, and Farrar & Maag, 2002) reported correlation between ToM and language within the range of .60 to .70 range. In general the findings indicated that language development and false belief understanding are relatively strongly related, even when the language measures were taken 1 or 2 years before children start mastering false belief tasks. However, none of these studies indicated the nature of the relationship between language and theory of mind. Astington and Jenkins (1995) raised two major questions regarding the relationship between a theory of mind and language: (a) how can we explain the relationship? and (b) what aspects of language are involved in theory of mind understanding? To answer the first question, they concluded, after reviewing a number of studies, that there is no clear or obvious answer to this question. They attempted to evaluate three possible relationships between ToM and language: (i) ToM depends upon language; (ii) language depends upon ToM and (iii) both are related to some other biological or socio-cultural variables. These issues are discussed below with reference to recent research in this area. Regarding the second question, they explained the relationship between pragmatics, semantics, and syntactic aspect, of language with theory of mind understanding. Studies that highlight the relationship between a theory of mind and the pragmatics, semantics, and syntactic aspect of language are reviewed in the following.

How Can we Expain the Relationship

Theory of Mind Depends upon Language

Research in this field indicated that language and conversation play a significant role in the development of a theory of mind (Harris, Rosnay & Pons, 2005):

(a) *It has been argued that linguistic ability is required for successful performance in a ToM task.* Usually in these tasks children are told stories that are enacted before them followed by some questions by the experimenter. These questions are primarily about the protagonist's mental state (what is he thinking?) and behaviour (where will he search for the object?) Chandler, Fritz, and Hala (1989) argued that 3-year-old children do understand false belief but that because of the linguistic complexity of the task they failed to show any understanding of theory of mind. However, attempt to simplify the language demand of the task didn't bring any success to children's performance. They can act out the doll's search behaviour (when the doll is holding a false belief) but they cannot make a verbal prediction of where the doll will look for the object. (Freeman, Lewis, & Doherty, 1991). Completely non-verbal tasks are even not easier than the standard tasks (Call & Tomasello,1999). These studies strongly support the hypothesis that ToM understanding depends upon language development, to the extent of linguistic expression of such an understanding.

(b) *Experimental language training studies* (Appleton & Reddy, 1996; Slaughter & Gopnik, 1996; Slaughter, 1998; Clements, Rustin & McCallum, 2000; Hale & Tager-Flusberg, 2003, and Lohmann & Tomasello, 2003) have special advantage that they are able to demonstrate causal relationship between children's language experience during training and later performance in ToM tasks. The finding from these studies claims that linguistic experience is a strong facilitator and perhaps a necessary condition for development of theory of mind understanding.

(c) *Research on atypical children (especially deaf and autistic children).* Deaf children born into non-signing families lag in theory of mind development. A causal link from language to theory of mind development is suggested by studies of deaf children born to hearing parents who have almost no available means of conversing with their parents during the early years of their life. They especially have limitation in conversing about mental states that have no obvious visual referent (de Villers & de Villers, 2000; Moeller & Schick, 2006; Peterson & Siegal, 1995, 1998, 1999, 2000). These children presumably experience the same number of situations as normally developing children in which they observe others in surprise reactions or experience their own false beliefs, but they struggle with false belief tasks up to the age of 16 years. In contrast, deaf children born to signing parents, who share a communicative system and thus have much richer linguistic experiences, develop concepts of false belief at the same age as the normal hearing children. Such children also had difficulty with non-verbal tasks. Moreover their performance in this task is predicted by their level of language development.

(d) *Exposure to maternal conversation rich in references to mental states promotes mental-state understanding.* Research with preschoolers indicate that parental use of mental state language plays an important role in the development of false belief (Cutting & Dunn,1999; Meins & Fernyhough, 1999; Ruffman, Slade & Crowe, 2002), emotion (Dunn, Brown, & Beardsall, 1991), and general theory of mind (Ruffman *et al.*, 2002) understanding. This issue will be discussed later.

(e) *Individual differences in development of theory of mind.* Recent empirical studies also reveal reliable individual differences of smaller magnitude among normally developing preschoolers in rates of mastering concepts of mind. Most of these studies discussed later (in chapter 4) indicated the role of language more specifically development of mental state vocabulary on theory of mind understanding.

Language Depends upon Theory of Mind

According to this view theory of mind develops prior to children's development of language. Children first acquire a conceptual understanding of false belief and appearance—reality distinction and then elaboration of language occurs to reflect upon such an understanding. This argument is consistent with Piaget's view that thought precedes language, a view that underlies much of cognitive development research. Such an argument is consistent with the proposal that false belief understanding is dependent on innate modular systems (Baron-Cohen, 1995; Leslie & Roth, 1993). It is also consonant with Perner's (1988) proposal that the child uses mental models to represent false belief. Adults loss of linguistic capacity does not led to lose of false belief understanding (Varley, 1998). Even then we cannot reject the role of language on theory of mind as theory of mind understanding might still be facilitated by language development.

Theory of Mind and Language Depend upon some other Factors

The correlation between theory of mind and language could be because both are the result of some other underlying endogenous (internal) or exogenous (external) factors. Some researchers (Zelazo & Jacques, 1996) viewed that development in executive function allow children to reason using complex embedded rules that are then exploited in both theory of mind and language performance. Other researchers (Dunn, 1996; Nelson, Plesa & Henseler, 1998) viewed that the child's increasingly sophisticated participation in social and cultural activities promote both theory of mind and language development. According to this view theory of mind and language development are intertwined, each promoting the development of the other *via* a bootstrapping mechanism.

What Aspects of Language are Involved in Theory of Mind?

The three aspects of language: syntax, semantics and pragmatics are strongly related in normal language development and probably so for development of theory of mind. The relationship of all the three aspects of language and theory of mind is worth examining.

Semantics and a Theory of Mind

At the semantic level, lexical terms are used to refer to mental states. The literature is rich with studies in English, French, Oriya, and other languages showing the development of mental terms and its relationship to development of a theory of mind. Before discussing these studies, an analysis of the relationship between mental state, speech act, and verbs referring to both the states is in order.

Mental states are expressed in speech acts which are the basic units of communication (Searle, 1969). Mental states and speech acts consist of attitudes to propositions. Mental states are considered as propositional attitudes which specify the relation between a content expressed by a proposition and its holder. Thus, attitudes denote the nature of a mental state, e.g. belief, desire, and intention (Table 2.1).

Table 2.1 : Examples of the relationship between subject, propositional attitude and proposition

Subject	*Attitude (type of mental state)*	*Proposition or content of mental state*
I	1. Think 2. Believe(s)	1. That the cup of coffee is hot 2. That the cup of coffee is hot
He	3. Want(s) 4. Intend	3. To have a hot cup of coffee 4. To ask for a cup of hot coffee

Though the proposition is the same, there is an obvious difference in believing it, wanting it, and intending it. Beliefs are either true or false in relation to reality. If the propositional content of a belief corresponds to the way things are in the world, then the belief is true and if it does not correspond, then the belief is false. In the latter case, one can change it by changing the belief. If the propositional content of desire or intention corresponds to reality, then it is fulfilled, otherwise it is unfulfilled. In order to fulfil one cannot change the desire, but the reality has to be changed. Thus, one's desires may cause changes in the world. In short, the evaluation of attitudes indicates the nature of the mental state. For example, the degree of certainly (truth or falsity) is indicated in the case of belief by using think, know or guess; similarly variations in strength in the case of desire or intention is indicated by using want, wish, need, etc. Thus, attitudes are mental state verbs that qualify the propositional content.

In the case of speech acts, the illocutionary force is indicated explicitly by the use of the speech act verb. A mental state and a speech act may have the same propositional content. For example, one can believe that "there are some biscuits in the cupboard" and say, "there are some biscuits in the cupboard" (speech act of assertion). The truth or falsity of the belief depends upon the fact whether there are biscuits in the cupboard or not, so also the truth or falsity of the statement. Most of the time our statements express our beliefs, our request indicates our desires, our promises reveal our intention (Astington, 1993).

Development of Mental State Words

Several attempts have been made to examine experimentally the understanding of the semantic distinction underlying different mental state words. The most commonly studied semantic property is that of presupposition. According to Kiparsky and Kiparsky (1970), certain verbs, including mental verbs know and remember presuppose the truth of the complement statement while other verbs, including mental verbs think and guess, do not. Verbs of the former kind are called factives and verbs of the latter kind are called non-factives. A term such as "know" can be differentiated from one such as "think" in that the former implies that the subject of the verb has unambiguous evidence, either perceptual or inferential, as to the truth of the complement, while the latter implies that the subject does not have such evidence. In some studies children had to comment on the truth value of statements drawn from either factive or non-factive contexts (Abbeduto & Rosenberg, 1985; Hopman & Maratsos, 1978; Mac Namara, Baker, & Olson, 1976; Scoville & Gordon, 1980). In other studies children were asked to select mental terms that best described a person's mental orientation to words, an event or an object. The correct choice was expected to reflect the understanding that the different terms required different evidential bases (Abbeduto & Rosenberg, 1985; Babu, 1989; Babu & Mishra, 2000; Johnson & Maratsos, 1977; Miscione, Marvin, O'Brien & Greenberg, 1978; Moore & Davidge, 1989; Moore, Harris & Patriquin, 1993; Wellman & Johnson, 1979). All these studies indicate that children do not start to differentiate between the verbs on the basis of their presupposition until 4-5 years of age. It is during this period that children also develop a concept of mind. The relationship between children's understanding of the presuppositions of think and know and their understanding of a concept of mind is evident in a number of studies among Oriya speaking children in India (Babu & Mishra, 2000; Pattnaik, 1997; Satpathy, 1993) and among English-speaking children (Moore, Pure, & Furrow, 1990). Bartsch and Wellman (1995) provided a comprehensive account of the naturalistic use of belief-desire terms during 18 months to 6 years of age and related the findings to studies on children's development of a theory of mind.

At a general level semantic ability facilitates verbal social interaction that in turn facilitates development of theory of mind (Dunn,1988, Nelson, 1996). Olson argued that mental terms such as "think", "know", and "remember" are used to talk about mental states. Mental states are unobservable, although their effects can be felt in self and other. These unobservable phenomena are brought to the child's attention when they are referred to with linguistic terms in day-to-day conversation. In general the idea is that these linguistic symbols are used by adults to indicate the relevant mental states, and so in learning the referents of these terms children form the relevant concepts in Whorfian fashion.

Syntactic Forms of Language

Syntactic ability is the ability to combine words to form sentences. The ability to form correct syntactic structure enables children to form representations of the reality. It was argued by de Villers (1995), de Villers and de Villers (2000) that the grammatical form of the way adults talk about beliefs and related mental states, provides children with a necessary representational format for dealing with false beliefs. Moreover, mental state reports require complex and embedded sentence structure, e.g., "Ritu thinks Reema is at home", "I know he will be coming home" or "He says that he will purchase a car". The embedded sentences " Reema is at home", "he will be coming home" or "he will purchase a car" forms a subordinate clause that act as the grammatical object of the verb "think", "know" and "say" in the main sentence. Such "object complements" are important here as they help us to report our mental representations. In reporting the false belief of another person the speaker can formulate a sentence where the whole sentence may be true even though the embedded sentence is false. Thus one can truthfully say "Ritu thinks the chocolate is in the cupboard" even though in reality the chocolate is in the drawer and the speaker is well aware of it. It is especially the realization of an open truth value of the embedded proposition (the fact that when Ritu thinks that Reema is home does not necessarily mean that Reema is really at home) that leads children in their understanding of epistemic states in people (de Villers & de Villers, 2000). The authors acknowledged that the semantics of the matrix mental state verbs may play some role as well, but the semantics and syntax in this case are closely related. The importance of the relationship between a theory of mind and children's mastery of the basic syntactic forms of their language, particularly object complement was suggested by Astington and Jenkins (1995). In a longitudinal study, they found that children with well-developed syntactic skills for referring to propositional contents or semantic terms for referring to propositional attitudes possessed the linguistic resources available to promote the development of a theory of mind. Though one can argue for a strong relationship between theory of mind task and syntactic task that use object complements, from the available data nothing can be conclusively stated regarding the direction of the relationship (Tager-Flusberg, 1997). The role of children's understanding of syntax of complementation in their understanding of ToM was indicated in a training study by Hale and Tager-Flusberg (2003). It was observed that children trained with sentential complement subsequently improved in their false belief understanding.

Pragmatics and a Theory of Mind

It is not just the knowledge of mental state verbs and sentence complement rather it is the use of language in context and the process of language interchange that children experience in discourse with other people which is important for development of a theory of mind. Harris (1996, 1999) claimed that it is in the to and fro of discourse that the child comes to appreciate that other people know things he or she does not know, that they do not know things they ought to know and they have different perspectives on things. Along these lines Tomasello (1999) stressed the importance of discourse interactions involving misunderstandings and requests for clarifications as particularly clear signals of peoples differing perspectives or understandings of the situations. This usage based or discourse based view also gets support from the correlational studies of Peterson and Siegal (1999, 2000). In their research, deaf children who had the opportunity to engage in richer discourse interactions with others were also more skilful in understanding false belief. However, the discourse interactions would definitely involve mental state word as well as complex syntax as we cannot talk about mind without using such words in complex syntactic structure. Most of the training studies have employed rich discourse interaction as part of their training. However, none could isolate the use of mental state words as well as sentential complement in their discourse training.

According to Lohmann and Tomasello (2003) both perspective-shifting discourse and sentential complement play important role in the ontogeny of theory of mind.

At a very early age, i.e., at 1 and 2 years, children's communicative abilities imply that they have a theory of mind (Bretherton, McNew & Beeghly-Smith, 1981). But at this age they cannot ascribe mental states to others. Although at this stage the intentional nature of communication is not explicit in their understanding of mental state. However, the general argument is that, since effective human interaction is not possible without an awareness of a theory of mind, language use is dependent on the development of a theory of mind. "Without a theory of mind, one cannot participate in a conversation" (de Gelder, 1987, p. 288).

Chapter-3
Existence of Mental State Vocabulary in Different Languages

Before studying the acquisition of mental state words and the contextual and group variations in use of such words it seems necessary to look at the existence of such words in the language in question. It is not that mental state words does not exist in every language, but there might be wide variations in use of such vocabulary by native speakers of different languages. Such differences would definitely determine the variability in the rate of acquisition of such words. A number of lists of mental state words in English language is available in the literature (e.g. Austin, 1962; Vendler, 1970). The motivation for investigating words of internal state has been discussed by Gearhart and Hall (1979; 1983) and elsewhere (cf. Wellman & Johnson, 1979). It is based on the following hypotheses:

(a) that the vocabulary in the internal state domain determines to a large extent the repertory of concepts in this area;
(b) that certain types of internal state word usage will correlate with skill in metacognitive processes;
(c) that therefore frequency of certain types of internal state word usage, and perhaps size of internal state word vocabulary, will correlate with greater readiness for, and success in, school; and
(d) that situational variation exists in the function and use of words of internal state (Hall, Nagy & Nottenburg, 1981)

Relevant Research Issues

At this point two major questions can be raised. They are :

(1) Is the acquisition of mental state vocabulary universal? That is: does the child acquire such vocabulary in the course of language development, irrespective of the language spoken by him/her; and the literacy environment and culture in which she/he is reared?

(2) The second question which follows from the first is: does the mental state words exist in the language spoken by the child or not? If such words exists, how they are used by the adult native speaker of that language? It is important to investigate this question prior to looking at the acquisition of such terms.

The use of internal state words or metarepresentational words is an issue to be considered at this point. Mental state can be experienced without being verbalised by use of any mental state words and mental state word can be uttered independent of any experience of such mental state. Thus there could be a discrepancy between use of internal state words and communication about internal states. People can talk about internal states without using internal state words and also use internal state words without any reference to internal state. This discrepancy is captured by what Hall and Nagy (1986) termed as "semantic-pragmatic" distinction. According to this view, an internal state word is considered "semantic" if it is used to refer to and hence to communicate about an internal state; it is considered "pragmatic" if the function in the sentence is something other than to communicate about internal states. In any normal conversation in English when someone says "Anita knows the answer", the intended meaning has something to do with Anita's knowledge. On the other hand when someone says "you know she is a good dancer", the intention is not to convey about knowledge as such. Rather, in the second case, "you know" is used as a conversational device or conversational postulates. These are highly stereotyped phrases containing internal state words which have completely or almost completely lost their internal content as in the example: "You know, I should do something about the repair of the car".

There are also a number of usages where the contribution of internal state word to the meaning of the utterance is diminished or made indirect by various conversational implicatures and conventions. Among these are indirect "requests" and "suggestions", such as "Do you want to take out the garbage, please" and Hedges, such as, "He is in his office, I think". So far, the discussion has focused on semantic/pragmatic distinctions in English. The question is does such distinction exist in other languages as well? Whether native Oriya speakers (one of the regional language of India) also use metarepresentational or mental state words the same way? In this chapter, a research on Oriya native speakers is discussed which would enable us to answer these questions.

According to Hall & Nagy (1986) there are four major sub-classes of mental state words: Cognitive (Know, remember, think, aware), Perceptual (see, hear, look, watch, feel), Affective (like, love, hope, hate, afraid), and Intentions and Desires (Want, Decide, Intend, Choose). Babu & Mamata (1992) in their research on literacy and mental state words of literate, illiterate and oral literate adults noted five categories of mental state words such as Cognitive, Perceptual, Affective, Intention/Desire and Linguistic.

Language Analysis: A Search for Mental State Words in Oriya

The purpose of the research reported in this section was to prepare a list of mental state words in Oriya with the frequencies of occurrence in different contexts (formal to informal, text book to novel etc.) and among varied groups of samples (like adults *versus* children, literate *versus.* semi-literate and illiterate). This study was conducted by following two different approaches for investigation of mental state words in Oriya language. The existing Oriya literature was surveyed in depth along with analysis of formal and informal conversations by Oriya adults and children covering a wide range of literacy levels.

Method

Design

The research was conducted under two phases: (1) literature survey, and (2) analysis of informal and formal discourse among native speakers of Oriya. The design of the research is given in Table 3.1.

Table 3.1: The design of the research

Method of observation		*Sample size*	*Age range*
1. Literature Survey		Dictionaries - 5 Epics - 5 Novels and other Literature - 5	
2. Recordings of formal and informal discourse such as : conversations, narration, professional discussion, debates, and public address	45	Illiterate adults	
	45	Literate adults	35yrs – 40yrs
	45	Semi-literate adults	
	84	Children out of which	
	42	Schooled	8yrs – 12yrs
	42	Unschooled	
	84	Total	

(a) *Literature survey* : An attempt was made to identify the mental state words, and note their frequencies of occurrence in a varied number of literatures such as: novels, essays, children's literature and text books (at primary and secondary levels) in Oriya language. In Indian Institute of Applied Language, Bhubaneswar, 3 million words from 63 categories has been collected and computer programme has been developed for finding out the frequencies and the context of use. This database was used to note down the frequencies of occurrence of the different mental state words along with the contextual variations. The research would focus on variations in use of mental state words across different age and grade levels, across different levels of literacy and in various contexts of use like formal discourse (like professional discussion, debates, etc.) to informal conversations.

(b) *Recording of formal and informal discourse*: An attempt was made to record the formal discourse such as professional discussions, debates etc. of literate samples and informal conversation of literate, semiliterate and illiterate adults. Further, informal conversations of schooled and unschooled children and adolescents were also recorded. These materials were processed in a computer to get the frequencies and contextual variations in use.

Sample

(a) Novels, biographies, essays, children's literature and text books from primary and secondary levels with at least 10 from each category constitute the sample for literature survey.

(b) Initially a group of approximately 200 adults were given an assessment of reading and writing and on the basis of their scores three categories of adults were taken for the study, i.e. literate (with highest range of scores), semi-literate (with average range of scores) and illiterate (with the lowest range of scores). There were 135 adults for the final sample with 45 per each category. Besides that 84, 8year, 10 year and 12 year olds with 14 schooled and 14 unschooled at each age level were also selected. The adults and children were selected from rural and semi-urban areas of Orissa around Cuttack and Khurda districts (Table 3.1).

Procedure

In order to investigate how metarepresentational words are used by native speakers of Oriya in oral and written communication of both causal and formal in nature, a group of 135 adults from 3 literacy levels and 84 schooled and unschooled children were studied. The natural conversations and narratives of all the groups were recorded. The investigator took initiative in beginning the conversation, which continued for approximately 30 minutes. All of them were asked to narrate a story. The literary conversations include such activities like debate, public address and professional discussion. The time span for each activity ranges from 30-60 minutes. The text obtained from the literature and the informal and formal conversations of the native speakers were considered for the final analysis.

Analysis and Interpretation

As stated earlier the purpose of this phase of the research was to prepare a list of mental state words in Oriya language, evaluating their frequencies in different contexts varying from adults to children and from formal to informal texts. For this purpose Oriya texts were obtained by literature survey and by field study. Written texts were obtained from published Oriya literature such as novels, essays, children's literature and text books. Oral texts were obtained from informal discussions, narrations, debates and professional discussions by Oriya speaking adults and children. The texts so obtained were analysed and mental state words occurring in them were noted along with their frequencies of occurrences. The criteria developed earlier by Babu and Mamata (1992) were followed for considering a word as a mental state word. The results obtained in this research are discussed separately for literature survey and field study.

Literature Survey

A brief summary of the findings of the literature survey is as follows:

(1) A list of mental state words in various texts with their frequencies is prepared (Table 3.2— Table 3.5).
(2) Comparison of the various texts shows that the varieties of words and their frequencies are more in adult texts compared to children's text (Table 3.6).

(3) Comparison of the different categories of mental state words shows that the most frequently occurred words are in the metacognitive and meta-affective category and least number of words are in the metaperceptual category irrespective of the differences in type of text (Table 3.7).

(4) Comparison of the different types of words shows that there are only few words such as: know, think, say, in each category, occurred most frequently in the different text types (Table 3.2—Table 3.5).

(5) So far as the different texts are concerned there is a difference in frequency of occurrence of mental state words. Such words have occurred most frequently in novels compared to essays and in children's literature compared to children's text books (Table 3.7). It is expected, as essays and children's text books are expository texts where as children's literature and novels are narratives. Narratives involve discussion of the protagonist's mental state (the level of consciousness) and the protagonist's action in the real world (level of action). Therefore, the occurrence of mental state words would be more frequent in these two categories of texts.

(6) Comparison of the different categories of mental state words among adults in three literacy levels and schooled and unschooled children shows that the most frequently occurred words are in the metalinguistic category followed by metacognitive, meta-affective and metaperceptual words.

(7) Comparison of the adults in three different literacy levels and schooled and unschooled children shows that the varieties of words and their frequencies are more among literate adults than semiliterate and illiterate adults. Similarly, frequency of occurrence and varieties of words are more among schooled children than unschooled children.

(8) Comparison of the different types of words reveals that the most frequently occurred words are only limited to 2 or 3 words in each category irrespective of variation in literacy and schooling.

(9) So far as the varieties of mental state words are concerned the most frequently occurred words are in the metacognitive and meta-affective category and least number of words are in the metalinguistic and metaperceptual category irrespective of the adults in three literacy levels and children.

Frequencies of Occurrence of Mental State Words

Metacognitive words

Consideration of the list of metacognitive words (Table 3.2) shows that there is not much difference in the frequencies of occurrence of 'know', 'think', 'understand', and 'mind' in the four different type, of text, i.e. adult's as well as children's text. The words, 'think' and 'know' with their various forms of elaboration are given in Table - 3.2. In *essays*: know, think, judge, intention, understanding, appear, belief, and in *novel*: know, think, intention, understanding, appear, remembering, accept, belief, mind are the most frequently occurred words. In *children's textbook*: know, think, understanding, mind, remembering and in *children's literature*: know, think, understanding, remembering, mind, forgetting, belief are the most frequently occurred words.

Table 3.2 : A list of Metacognitive words with their frequencies in each of the four different types of Oriya literature

Words	*Essays*	*Novels*	*Text Books*	*Children's Literature*
1. Know	76	79	67	66
2. Think	56	136	55	99
3. Judge	27	7	9	5
4. Intention	38	20	-	3
5. Understanding	50	44	46	79
6. Admit	17	4	-	-

(Contd...)

(**Table 3.2** : Contd...)

7. Confirm	11	-	-	-
8. Imagine	15	7	4	3
9. Appear	22	21	10	6
10. Pretend	4	1	1	2
11. Guess	4	-	1	-
12. Idea	8	17	-	1
13. Remembering	6	27	12	16
14. Forgetting	3	12	9	13
15. Analysis	3	-	-	-
16. Contradict	1	7	-	-
17. Aware	4	2	-	1
18. Doubt	11	17	-	8
19. Prove	-	4	-	-
20. Decide	9	16	-	1
21. Accept	9	23	-	5
22. Confuse	5	-	-	-
23. Sure	7	7	-	-
24. Conclude	3	9	-	-
25. Inspire	3	1	-	-
26. Belief	21	34	8	16
27. Mind	8	49	62	26
28. Compare	5	2	-	-
29. Truth	6	4	-	-
30. Lie	2	4	3	3
31. Intelligence	4	-	5	2
32. Consciousness	5	1	-	-
33. Puzzling	5	3	-	-
34. Discover	2	2	-	-
35. Concentrate	1	1	3	4
36. Study	2	-	2	-
37. Hesitate	3	3	-	-
38. Reading	6	12	4	-
39. Evaluate	3	-	-	-
40. Conscience	7	1	-	1
41. Clever	-	-	-	-
42. Alert	-	1	-	1
43. Insist	-	9	-	-
44. Attitude	-	4	-	-
45. Figureout	3	-	-	4
46. Learn	-	-	2	4
47. Patience	-	2	-	4
48. Dream	1	13	1	5
49. fool	-	-	-	-
50. Recognition	-	-	1	-

Metalinguistic Words

Table 3.3 shows that the two words that occurred most frequently in the four different texts are 'say' and 'ask'. In *essays*: say, ask, discuss, express and in *novels*: say, ask, answer, request are the most frequently occurred words. In *children's text books* and *literature* 'say' is the only frequently occurring metalinguistic word.

Table 3.3 : A list of Metalinguistic words with their frequencies in each of the four types of literature

Words	*Essays*	*Novels*	*Text Books*	*Children's Literature*
1. Say	120	291	36	83
2. Ask	21	31	1	5
3. Declare	10	7	-	-
4. Discuss	17	8	1	-
5. Describe	12	2	-	-
6. Mean	11	5	-	-
7. Mention	7	-	-	-
8. Address	5	6	-	-
9. Explain	9	3	3	-
10. Question	7	13	-	-
11. Order	6	11	-	-
12. Direct	5	4	-	-
13. Promise	4	8	-	-
14. Praise	3	8	8	10
15. Answer	8	26	-	-
16. Argue	4	3	-	-
17. Opinion	7	5	3	2
18. Request	1	14	-	-
19. Blame	1	4	-	-
20. Example	6	-	-	-
21. Advice	5	1	1	-
22. Persuade	1	-	-	-
23. Expression	14	2	-	1
24. Suggest	-	7	-	-
25. Complain	-	4	-	-
26. Remark	-	6	-	2
27. Threaten	-	-	1	-
28. Conversation	-	-	-	2

Meta-affective Words

In contrast to the above two categories, there are a number of meta-affective words that are more frequent in almost all types of text. These words are: feel, desire, hope, surprise, afraid. In *novels*: feel, desire, surprise, hope, love, joy, afraid, happy, shy, pain, sorrow, insult, anger, hesitate and in *essays*: feel, desire and hope are the most frequently occurred words. In *children's textbook:* desire, joy, happy, and in *children's literature*: desire, surprise, joy, afraid, happy, sorrow, angry are the most frequently occurred words (Table 3.4).

Table 3.4: Frequencies of Meta-affective words in each of the four categories of Oriya literature

Words	*Essays*	*Novels*	*Text Books*	*Children's Literature*
1. Feel	44	24	3	12
2. Desire	46	61	11	33
3. Surprise	13	29	9	29
4. Hope	23	20	7	12
5. Love	13	18	3	8
6. Joy	13	16	2	34
7. Distress	12	12	-	-
8. Afraid	11	25	9	28
9. Courage	8	11	-	-
10. Encourage	1	1	1	-
11. Happy	8	37	10	42
12. Jealousy	4	7	-	2
13. Disgust	7	8	3	5
14. Hurt	4	-	-	-
15. Worry	7	9	3	4
16. Shy	3	35	1	1
17. Pain	7	18	6	7
18. Sorrow	9	49	17	24
19. Interest	7	5	2	4
20. Satisfaction	8	5	-	8
21. Curiosity	1	2	-	-
22. Excite	1	7	-	-
23. Anxiety	1	6	-	7
24. Hate	2	10	2	1
25. Insult	1	30	-	-
26. Pathos	2	2	-	-
27. Grateful	4	3	-	-
28. Sympathy	4	5	-	1
29. Frustration	2	2	1	1
30. Startle	1	5	2	-

(Contd...)

(**Table 3.4** : Contd...)

31. Angry	3	24	5	16
32. Experience	2	2	-	-
33. Affection	2	1	-	1
34. Cruel	1	-	-	-
35. Like	1	-	5	4
36. Indifferent	2	3	-	-
37. Console	2	5	1	3
38. Devotion	6	-	-	1
39. Pride	5	9	3	2
40. Emotional	2	2	-	-
41. Hesitate	3	15	-	1
42. Attract	5	4	-	-
43. Mourn	-	4	-	1
44. Tired	-	3	3	-
45. Greed	-	7	-	2
46. Sacrifice	-	5	-	-
47. Repent	-	5	1	-
48. Forgive	-	10	-	-
49. Mercy	-	6	-	-
50. Stunned	-	4	4	12
51. Agitate	-	1	-	-
52. Confuse	2	4	3	1
53. Peace	5	6	3	-
54. Calm	5	4	-	-
55. Enthusiasm	4	-	1	1

Metaperceptual Words

As is evident from Table - 3.5, the most frequently occurred metaperceptual words are 'see' and 'hear'.

Table 3.5 : Frequency of Metaperceptual words in each of the four categories of oriya literature

Words	*Essays*	*Novels*	*Text Books*	*Children's Literature*
1. See	118	121	5	42
2. Hearing	19	24	11	10
3. Notice	7	7	-	-
4. Search	5	1	-	-
5. Observe	2	-	-	-
6. Smell	1	-	-	-

Lexical Elaboration of Mental State Words

The lexical elaboration in this context refers to the set of synonymous words under each of the category of mental state words. The words in these categories would probably vary in complexity, frequency of use and in acquisition. The lexical elaboration of the different mental state words as obtained from the literature survey are given in (Table 3.8a,b,c,d; 3.9a,b,c,d).

Table 3.6 : Varieties of mental state words under each category in the different Oriya literature

Category	*Essay*	*Novel*	*Text Book*	*Children's Literature*
Meta-affective	46	50	29	33
Metacognitive	41	38	20	26
Metalinguistic	23	23	9	7
Metaperceptual	6	4	2	2

Table 3.7 : Percentage of occurrence of the different categories of mental state words in the various types of Oriya literature

Category	*Essay*	*Novel*	*Text Book*	*Children's Literature*
Total No. of words	41064	36736	28716	23318
Metacognitive	1.15	1.64	1.06	1.62
Meta-affective	.77	1.59	.42	1.32
Metalinguistic	.69	1.27	.18	.45
Metaperceptual	.37	.42	.05	.22

Table 3.8a : Lexical elaboration of meta-affective and metacognitive words and their frequencies in Children's Literature

Sl. No.	*Meta-affective Words*	*Lexical Elaboration and Frequencies of Oriya words*	*Sl. No.*	*Meta-cognitive Words*	*Lexical Elaboration and Frequencies of Oriya Words*
1.	Desire	*Echha(V)(23)* *Chahein (V) (7)* *Mana Baleiba(V) (1)* *Aakankhya (N) (1)* *Manobanchha (N) (1)*	1.	Understand	*Bujhiba(V)(79)*
2.	Astonished/Surprised	*Aascharya Heba (V) (20)* *Bismita Heba (V) (9)*	2.	Think	*Bhabana* *Bhabiba (N) (1)* *Manobhaba (N) (3)* *Mane Kariba (V) (8)* *Chinta Kariba (V) (25)* *Chinta Magna (N) (1)* *Chintita (N) (1)*
3.	Happy	*Khusi (V) (25)* *Sukha (N) (9)* *Prasanna(V) (1)* *Thatta/Majja(V) (7)*	3.	Belief	*Biswas Kariba (V) (16)*
4.	Fear	*Bhaya (V) (13)* *Aatanka (N) (2)* *Dara/Chhania(V) (5)* *Bhayabita(V) (5)* *Aasanka (N) (2)* *Katara (V) (1)*	4.	Knowledge/Know	*Janiba (V) (54)* *Gyana (N) (8)* *Jigyansa (N) (1)* *Bodha (V) (3)*

(Contd...)

(**Table 3.8a** : Contd...)

5. Stunned	*Mugdha Heba(V) (9)* *Tatasta (V) (1)* *Stambibhuta (V) (1)* *Bimohita (V) (1)*	5. Mind	*Mana (N) (26)*
6. Disgust	*Birakta Heba (V) (5)*	6. Forget	*Bhulijiba(V) (11)*
7. Jealousy	*Ersha Kariba (V) (1)* *Hinsa (V) (1)*	7. Remember	*Mane Padila Nahin(V) (2)* *Mane Pakaiba(V) (12)* *Smarana Kariba (V)(4)*
8. Sorrow	*Duukha Kariba (V) (18)* *Duukhita Heba (V) (4)* *Mana Kharap Kariba (V) (1)* *Pratarita (V) (1)*	8. Alert	*Satarka (V)(1)*
9. Mourn	*Shoka Kariba (V) (1)*	9. Aware	*Sachetana (V)(1)*
10. Feel	*Anubhaba Kariba (V) (11)* *Lagiba (V) (1)*	10. Learn	*Sikhiba(V) (3)* *Sikhya (N) (1)*
11. Joy	*Aananda Heba (V) (34)*	11. Figure-out	*Dharineba(V) (4)*
12. Like	*Pasanda Kariba (V) (3)* *Aasakti (N) (1)*	12. Intelligence	*Buddhi (N) (2)*
13. Love	*Bhala Pae (V) (5)* *Priya (N) (2)* *Prema (N) (1)*	13. Concentration	*Dhhyana (N) (3)* *Manadei(V) (1)*
14. Affection	*Mamata (N) (1)*	14. Patience	*Dhairya (N) (3)* *Byakula (V)(1)*

(Contd...)

(**Table 3.8a** : Contd...)

15. Interest	*Aagrahi Heba (V) (4)*	15.	Intention	*Lakhya (N) (2)*
				Uddesya (N) (1)
16. Anxiety	*Udbigna (V) (5)*	16.	Doubt	*Sandeha (V) (8)*
	Utkanthita (V) (2)			
17. Enthusiasm	*Uschahita Heba (V) (1)*	17.	Dream	*Swapna (N) (5)*
18. Satisfaction	*Santusta Heba (V) (6)*	18.	Pretence	*Chhalana (V) (2)*
	Trupti (N) (2)			
19. Sympathy	*Sahanubhuti (N) (1)*	19.	Lie	*Michha Katha (N) (2)*
				Mithya (V) (1)
20. Shy	*Lajja (N) (1)*	20.	Appear	*Mane Heba (V) (6)*
21. Worry	*Byasta Heba (V) (3)*	21.	Conscience	*Bibeka (N) (1)*
	Byastata (N) (1)			
22. Hate	*Ghruna Kariba (V) (1)*	22.	Imagine	*Kalpana Kariba (V) (3)*
23. Confuse	*Bichalita Heba (V) (1)*	23.	Idea	*Dharana Kariba (V) (1)*
24. Anger	*Ragiba (V) (7)*	24.	Judge	*Bichara Kariba (V) (5)*
	Krodha Kariba (V) (7)			
	Rodha Kariba (V) (1)			
	Ragare (N) (1)			
25. Console	*Santwana Deba (V) (2)*	25.	Decide	*Manasta Kariba (V) (1)*
	Aaswasta Kariba (V) (1)			
26. Proud	*Garba (V) (1)*	26.	Accept	*Maniba (V) (5)*
	Ahankara (N) (1)			
27. Hope	*Aasaa Kariba (V) (11)*			
	Nirasa Heba (V) (1)			

(Contd...)

(Table 3.8a : Contd...)

28. Greed	*Lobha Kariba (V) (1)*
	Pralobhana (N) (1)
29. Pain	*Kasta Heba/Deba (V) (5)*
	Jantrana (V) (2)
30. Frustrated	*Hatas Heba (V)(1)*
31. Hesitance	*Sankocha Kariba (V) (1)*
32. Devotion	*Bhakti (N) (1)*
33. Expression	*Bhaba (V) (3)*

Table 3.8 b : Lexical elaboration of meta-affective and metacognitive words and their frequencies in children's text books

Sl. No.	*Meta-affective Words*	*Lexical Elaboration and Frequencies of Oriya Words*	*Sl. No.*	*Meta-cognitive Words*	*Lexical Elaboration and Frequencies of Oriya Words*
1.	Desire	*Echha Kariba/Heba (V) (7)* *Kamana Kariba (V) (1)* *Chahinba (V)(3)*	1.	Think	*Bhabiba (V) (22)* *Bhabana (N) (6)* *Manobhaba (V) (4)* *Chinta Kariba (V) (12)* *Chintadhara (N) (6)* *Manobrutti (V) (5)* *Bichar Kariba (V)(9)*
2.	Happy	*Khusi Heba (V) (4)* *Sukha (N) (5)* *Mauja Kariba (V) (1)*	2.	Judge	
3.	Joy	*Ananda (N) (2)* *Manasika (N) (1)*	3.	Mind	*Mana (N) (61)*
4.	Like	*Bhala Lagiba (V) (4)* *Manamatania (N) (1)*	4.	Knowledge	*Janiba (V) (61)* *Gyana (N) (4)* *Bodha (N) (2)*
5.	Love	*Bhala Paiba (V) (3)*	5.	Understand	*Bujhiba (V) (46)*
6.	Sorrow	*Duukha (N) (2)* *Duukha Heba (V) (15)*	6.	Read	*Padhiba (V) (4)*
7.	Worry	*Byasta Heba (V) (2)* *Nischinta Heba (V)(1)*	7.	Intelligence	*Buddhi (V) (5)*
8.	Expression	*Bhaba (N) (4)*	8.	Remember	*Mane Padiba (V) (12)*
9.	Fear	*Dara Lagiba (V) (4)* *Bhaya (N) (3)* *Aashanka (N) (2)*	9.	Lie	*Michha (N) (3)*

(Contd...)

(**Table 3.8b** : Contd...)

10. Disgust	*Birakta Heba (V) (3)*	10. Forget	*Bhulijiba (V) (7)*
			Hetunahin (V) (2)
11. Encouragement	*Uschahita Heba (V)(1)*	11. Belief	*Biswas Kariba (V) (7)*
			Aatma Biswas (N)(1)
12. Frustration	*Hatasa Heba (V) (1)*	12. Guess	*Anuman (V) (1)*
13. Anger	*Krodha (N) (1)*	13. Concentration	*Dhyana (V) (1)*
	Raga (N) (4)		*Manadei (V) (2)*
14. Peace	*Shanti (N) (3)*	14. Recognise	*Chinhila (V) (1)*
15. Repent	*Anutapa kariba (V) (1)*	15. Study	*Adhayana Kariba (V) (2)*
16. Surprised/Astonished	*Chamakruta Heba (V) (1)*	16. Learn	*Sikhi (V) (2)*
	Aascharya Heba (V) (5)		
	Bishmita Heba (V) (3)		
17. Pain	*Kasta (N) (5)*	17. Appear	*Mane Heba (V) (10)*
	Bedana (N) (1)		
18. Hate	*Ghruna (N) (2)*	18. Imagination	*Kalpana Kariba (V) (4)*
19. Shy	*Lajja (N) (1)*	19. Pretence	*Chalana (N) (1)*
20. Stunned	*Mugdha Heba (V) (4)*	20. Dream	*Swapna (N) (1)*
21. Tired	*Klanta (N) (3)*		
22. Interest	*Aagraha (N) (2)*		
23. Confuse	*Bichalita Heba (V) (3)*		
24. Proud	*Garva (N) (1)*		
	Ahankar (N) (2)		
25. Feel	*Anubhab Kariba (V) (3)*		
26. Enthusiasm	*Uschaha (N) (1)*		
27. Hope	*Aasha Kariba (V) (7)*		
28. Startled	*Chamaki Padiba (V) (2)*		
29. Console	*Sahanubhuti Dekhaiba (V) (1)*		

Table 3.8c : Lexical elaboration of meta-affective and metacognitive words and their frequencies in oriya novel

Sl. No.	*Meta-affective Words*	*Lexical Elaboration and Frequencies of Oriya Words*	*Sl. No.*	*Meta-cognitive Words*	*Lexical Elaboration and Frequencies of Oriya Words*
1.	Feel	*Anubhaba Kariba (V) (18)* *Anubhuta Heba (V) (1)* *Anubhuti (N) (2)* *Anubhaba (N) (3)*	1.	Know	*Janiba (V) (70)* *Bujhi Pariba (V) (7)* *Jigyansa (N) (2)*
2.	Desire	*Eccha Kariba/Heba (V)(9)* *Chahinba (V) (29)* *Kamana Kariba (V) (1)* *Bancha Kariba (V) (1)* *Mana Kariba/Heba (V) (3)* *Echha (N) (12)* *Kamana (N) (4)* *Abhipraya (N) (1)* *Aakankhya (N) (1)*	2.	Think	*Bhabiba (V) (94)* *Bhabana (N) (1)* *Chinta (N) (15)* *Chintita (N) (2)* *Chinta Kariba (V) (4)* *Chintita Heba (V) (2)* *Mane Kariba(V) (7)* *Maniba (V)* *Sumari (V) (1)(3)*
3.	Sorrow	*Duukha (N) (32)* *Duukhi Heba (V) (1)* *Duukhita (N) (3)* *Bisarna Heba (V) (3)* *Bisarna (N) (1)* *Udasa (N) (1)* *Bisada (N) (1)* *Khyobha (N) (3)* *Abasosa (N) (1)*	3.	Judge	*Bichara Kariba (V) (3)* *Bichara (N) (4)*

(Contd...)

(**Table 3.8c** : Contd...)

		Abasosa Rahiba (V)(1) *Khyuma Heba(V) (2)*			
4.	Excited	*Uttejana (N) (5)* *Uttejita Heba (V) (2)*	4.	Intention	*Uddesya (N) (6)* *Lakhya (N) (5)* *Chesta (N) (2)* *Chesta Kariba (V) (6)* *Udyama Kariba (V) (1)*
5.	Insult	*Apaman (N) (12)* *Apamanita (N) (1)* *Apamana Kariba (V) (3)* *Apamanita Kariba (V) (7)* *Lanchana (N) (6)* *Lanchhita Heba (V) (1)*	5.	Understand	*Bujhiba (V) (43)* *Abujha (N) (1)*
6.	Anxiety	*Udbega (N) (3)* *Udbigna (N) (1)* *Udbigna Heba (V) (2)*	6.	Hesitate	*Dwanda (N) (3)*
7.	Hesitate	*Kuntha (N) (3)* *Kunthita (N) (4)* *Kunthita Heba (V) (2)* *Kuntha Kariba (V) (2)* *Sankocha (N) (3)*	7.	Imagine	*Kalpana Kariba (V) (2)* *Kalpana (N) (5)*
8.	Mourn	*Akuntha (N) (1)* *Shoka (N) (2)* *Shokavivuta (N) (2)*	8.	Doubt	*Sandeha Kariba (V) (4)* *Aasanka Kariba (V) (1)*

(Contd...)

(Table 3.8c : Contd...)

			Sansaya Prakasa Kariba (V) (1)
			Sandeha (N) (6)
			Aasanka (N) (3)
			Sansaya (N) (2)
9. Afraid	*Bhaya (N) (9)*	9. Concentrate	*Tanmaya Heba (V) (1)*
	Bhaya Heba/Kariba (V) (6)		
	Dariba (V) (6)		
	Dara (N) (1)		
	Aatanka (N) (2)		
	Santrasta (N) (1)		
10. Pain	*Jantrana (N) (2)*	10. Alert	*Satarka (N) (1)*
	Kasta (N) (5)		
	Kasta Paiba/Lagiba (V) (5)		
	Jatana (N) (1)		
	Klesa (N) (1)		
	Bedana (N) (3)		
	Byatha Paiba (V) (1)		
11. Happy	*Khusi (N) (5)*	11. Inspire	*Anupranita Kariba (V) (1)*
	Khusi Heba(V) (5)		
	Sukha (N) (10)		
	Sukhi Heba/Kariba (V)(8)		
	Sukhi (N) (3)		
	Utfhulla Heba (V) (4)		
	Ullasita Heba (V) (1)		
	Ullasa (N) (1)		

(Contd...)

(Table 3.8c : Contd...)

12. Tired	*Klanta (N) (1)* *Klanta Hoijiba (V) (2)*	12. Remember	*Smarana Kariba (V) (5)* *Mane Padiba (V) (14)* *Mane Rahiba (V) (1)* *Mane Pakaiba (V) (1)* *Smarana (N) (2)* *Smruti (N) (4)*
13. Shy	*Lajja (N) (17)* *Lajja Kariba (V) (1)* *Abhiman (N) (16)* *Abhiman Kariba (V) (3)*	13. Forget	*Bhulijiba (V) (10)* *Pasorijiba (V) (1)* *Abismaraniya (N) (1)*
14. Surprise	*Aascharya Heba (V) (6)* *Aascharya (N) (6)* *Bismaya (N) (4)* *Bishmit Heba (V) (1)* *Aachambita Heba (V) (1)* *Chakita Heba (V)(1)* *Chakita Bhaba (N) (1)* *Abak Hoijiba (V)(3)* *Bimudha Hoijiba (V) (1)* *Stabdha Heba (V) (3)* *Stambibhuta Heba(V) (2)*	14. Appear	*Mane Heba (V) (21)*
15. Distress	*Bibrata (N) (2)* *Bibrata Heba (V)(1)* *Byakula (N) (4)*	15. Sure	*Nischaya (N) (7)*

(Contd...)

(**Table 3.8c** : Contd...)

	Byakula Heba (V) (2) *Aakula Heba (V) (1)* *Byatibyasta Heba (V) (1)* *Byathita (N) (1)*		
16. Hope	*Aasha Kariba (V) (6)* *Aasha (N) (14)*	16. Contradict	*Birodha Kariba (V) (2)* *Birodhi (N) (5)*
17. Courage	*Sahasa Kariba (V) (6)* *Sahasa (N) (4)* *Dambha (N) (1)*	17. Mind	*Mana (N) (37)* *Mane Mane (N) (12)*
18. Hate	*Ghruna Kariba (V) (8)* *Ghruna (N) (2)*	18. Accept	*Maniba (V) (23)*
19. Startle	*Chamaki Padiba (V) (5)*	19. Conclude	*Siddhanta Kariba (V) (3)* *Siddhanta (N) (6)*
20. Disgust	*Birakta Heba (V) (4)* *Birakti (N) (4)*	20. Lie	*Mithya (N) (4)*
21. Greed	*Lobha (N) (4)* *Lobha Dekhaiba (V) (1)* *Pralobhita Kariba (V) (1)* *Lobhatur Heba (V) (1)*	21. Truth	*Satya (N) (4)*
22. Grateful	*Krutagnya Heba (V) (2)* *Krutagnyata (N) (1)*	22. Discover	*Aabishkara Kariba (V) (2)*
23. Pride	*Garva (N) (2)* *Ahankar (N) (7)*	23. Admit	*Sweekar Kariba (V) (4)*
24. Love	*Sneha (N) (6)* *Prema (N) (6)* *Bhala Paiba (V) (6)*	24. Idea	*Dharana Heba (V) (8)* *Dharana (N) (9)*

(Contd...)

(**Table 3.8c** : Contd...)

25. Sacrifice	*Tyaga (N) (5)*	25.	Decide	*Stira Kariba (V) (11)* *Manasta Kariba (V) (1)* *Thik Kariba (V) (3)* *Nispatti Neba (V) (1)*
26. Repent	*Anutapa (N) (2)* *Paschatapa (N) (1)* *Anutapa Heba (V) (1)* *Anusochana Heba(V) (1)*	26.	Insist	*Jid Kariba (V) (2)* *Jigara Kariba (V) (1)* *Ajhata Kariba (V) (1)* *Ali Kariba (V) (1)* *Jid (N) (3)* *Jigara (N) (1)*
27. Sympathy	*Sahanubhuti (N) (2)* *Samabedana (N) (1)* *Karuna (N) (2)*	27.	Conscience	*Bibeka (N) (1)*
28. Forgive	*Khyama* *Kariba/Magiba (V)(8)* *Khyama (N) (2)*	28.	Believe	*Biswas Kariba (V) (12)* *Bharasa Kariba (V) (1)* *Patyaya Aasiba (V) (1)* *Bharasa (N) (2)* *Biswas (N) (15)* *Abiswas (N) (2)* *Aasta (N) (1)*
29. Mercy	*Daya Kariba(V) (1)* *Daya (N) (3)* *Anukampa (N) (2)*	29.	Compare	*Tulana Kariba (V) (1)* *Tulana (N) (1)*
30. Attract	*Aakarshana Kariba (V) (1)* *Aakarshana (V) (1)*	30.	Prove	*Pramana Kariba (V) (2)* *Pramanita Kariba (V) (2)*

(Contd...)

(**Table 3.8c** : Contd...)

	Manalova (N) (1) *Aakrusta Heba (V)(1)*		
31. Angry	*Krodha (N) (6)* *Raga (N) (9)* *Ragiba (V) (6)* *Bigidiba (V) (2)* *Chidijiba (V) (1)*	31. Puzzle	*Rahasya (N) (2)* *Maya (N) (1)*
32. Joy	*Aananda (N) (10)* *Aanandita (N) (2)* *Aanandita Heba (V) (1)* *Aananda Deba/Paiba/ Kariba (V) (3)*	32. Consciousness	*Chetana (N) (1)*
33. Interest	*Aagraha (N) (3)* *Aagrahi (N) (1)* *Aagraha Kariba (V) (1)*	33. Aware	*Sachetana Kariba (V) (1)* *Sachetana Heba (V) (1)*
34. Experience	*Abhigyanta (N) (2)*	34. Pretend	*Prahasana (N) (1)*
35. Calm	*Santa (N) (2)* *Santa Bhabare (V) (1)* *Stitapragnya (N) (1)*	35. Read	*Padhiba (V) (12)*
36. Satisfaction	*Trupti (N) (3)* *Santusta Kariba (V) (1)* *Tusta Kariba (V) (1)*	*36. Attitude*	*Manobhaba (N) (4)*
37. Frustration	Hatasa Heba (V) (2)	37. Dream	Swapna (N) (11) *Swapna Dekhiba (V) (2)*

(Contd...)

(**Table 3.8c** : Contd...)

38. Worry	*Byasta Heba (V) (4)*	*38. Patience*	*Dhairya (N) (2)*
	Nischinta (N) (4)		
	Nischinta Heba (V)(1)		
39. Curious	*Kautuhala (N) (2)*		
40. Affection	*Mamata (N) (1)*		
41. Encourage	Uschahita Heba (V) (1)		
42. Pathos	Karuna (N) (2)		
43. Jealousy	Ersha (N) (5)		
	Ersha Kariba (V) (1)		
	Asuya (N) (1)		
44. Peace	Santi (N) (5)		
	Santi Paiba (V) (1)		
45. Stunned	Bihwalita Heba (V) (1)		
	Bimugdha Heba (V) (2)		
	Bimohita Heba (V) (1)		
46. Confuse	Bichalita Heba/Kariba (V) (2)		
	Bichalita (N) (2)		
47. Console	Aaswasta Heba (V) (2)		
	Santwana Deba (V) (2)		
	Prabodhana Deba (V) (1)		
48. Agitate	Aalodana (N) (1)		
49. Indifference	Udasina Heba (V) (1)		
	Udasa (N) (2)		
50. Emotional	Bhabaprabana Heba (V) (2)		

Table 3.8d : Lexical Elaboration of Meta-affective and Metacognitive words and their Frequencies in Oriya essays

Sl. No.	*Meta-affective Words*	*Lexical Elaboration and Frequencies of Oriya Words*	*Sl. No.*	*Meta-cognitive Words*	*Lexical Elaboration and Frequencies of Oriya Words*
1.	Feel	*Anubhaba Kariba (V) (24)* *Anubhuta Heba (V) (5)* *Anubhaba (N) (10)* *Anubhuti (N) (4)* *Hrutsparsh (V) (1)*	1.	Know	*Janiba (V) (42)* *Gochara Achi (V) (1)* *Bidida Achi (V) (1)* *Jigyansa (N) (1)* *Gyana (N) (17)* *Agyanta (N) (3)* *Gochara (N) (2)* *Gyanta Bhabare (N) (7)* *Anusandhana (N) (1)* *Anusandhista (N) (1)*
2.	Desire	*Echha Kariba (V) (8)* *Mana Kariba (V) (6)* *Spruhaniya Mane- Kariba (V) (2)* *Kamana Kariba (V) (1)* *Abhilas Kariba (V)(1)* *Aakankhya (N) (10)* *Aakankhya Kariba (V)(4)* *Abhi Praya (N) (1)* *Abhilipsa (N) (1)* *Banchaniya (N) (1)* *Spruhaniya (N) (1)* *Echha (N) (4)*	2.	Think *Mane Kariba (V) (13)*	*Bhabiba (V) (17)* *Chinta Kariba (V) (4)* *Gyana Kari (V) (3)* *Maniba (V) (7)* *Panchiba (V) (3)* *Bhaliba (V) (1)* *Chinta (N) (8)*

(Contd...)

(**Table 3.8d** : Contd...)

	Echhuka Heba (V) (1)		
	Prabrutti Heba (V) (1)		
	Lalsa (N) (2)		
	Pipasa (N) (2)		
3. Hope	*Aasha Kariba (V) (7)*	3. Judge	*Bichara Kariba (V) (6)*
	Pratyaasa Kariba (V) (1)		*Bichara (N) (20)*
	Aasha (N) (11)		*Pranidhana Kariba (V) (1)*
	Nairasya (N) (2)		
	Pratyaasa (N) (1)		
	Aasaprada (V)(1)		
4. Enthusiasm	*Uschaha (N) (4)*	4. Evaluate	*Mulyayana Kariba (V) (3)*
5. Encourage	*Uschahita Kariba (V) (1)*	5. Guess	*Anumana (N) (4)*
6. Surprise	*Aascharya Heba (V) (1)*	6. Idea	*Dharana Heba (V) (1)*
	Bismita Heba (V) (3)		*Dharana (N) (7)*
	Chakita Heba (V) (1)		
	Abak Heba (V) (1)		
	Stambibhuta Heba (V) (1)		
	Aachambita Heba (V) (1)		
	Bismaya (N) (4)		
	Aascharya (N) (1)		
7. Love	*Bhala Paiba (V) (4)*	7. Contradict	*Birodha Kariba (V) (1)*
	Sneha (N) (5)		
	Prema (N) (4)		

(Contd...)

(Table 3.8d : Contd...)

8. Happy	*Sukha (N) (6)* *Harsha (N) (1)* *Prasannata (N) (1)*	8. Pretend	*Chhalana (N (1)* *Chhalana Kariba (V) (1)* *Bheliki (N) (1)* *Prabanchana (N) (1)*
9. Jealousy	*Ersha (N) (3)* *Ersha Heba (V) (1)*	9. Intention	*Uddeshya (N) (16)* *Lakhya (N) (2)* *Abhista (N) (1)* *Udyama (N) (5)* *Chesta (N) (4)* *Chesta Kariba (V) (5)* *Udyama Kariba (V) (1)* *Prayyasa Kariba (V) (1)* *Jatna Kariba (V) (1)* *Prayyasa (N) (1)* *Aabhimukhya (N) (1)*
10. Distress	*Byathita Heba (V) (2)* *Byatibyasta Heba (V) (1)* *Aakula (N) (4)* *Bibrata (N) (2)* *Durdasa (N) (3)*	10. Remember	*Smarana Kariba (V) (1)* *Mane Rakhiba (V) (2)* *Smarana (N) (2)* *Smruti (N) (1)*
11. Worry	*Nischinta (N) (3)* *Byasta (N) (1)* *Nischinta Heba (V) (2)* *Nirbikara Bhabare (V) (1)*	11. Forget	*Bhulijiba (V) (1)* *Bismrusa Heba (V) (1)* *Bismarana (N) (1)*

(Contd...)

(Table 3.8d : Contd...)

12. Disgust 13. Hurt 14. Shy 15. Pain	*Birakti (N) (7)* *Tarjama Kariba (V) (1)* *Bislesana (N) (1)* *Aaghat Deba/Lagiba (V) (3)* *Marmahata Heba (V) (1)* *Lajja (N) (3)* *Jantrana (N) (1)* *Kasta (N) (2)* *Kasta Paiba (V) (3)* *Atista Hoipadiba (V) (1)*	12. Analysis 13. Aware 14. Accept 15. Inspire	*Bislesana Kariba (V) (1)* *Schetana Heba / Kariba (V) (2)* *Sachetana (N) (2)* *Maniba (V) (9)* *Prerana Deba (V) (2)* *Prerita Heba (V) (1)*
16. Curiosity	*Koutuhalaprada (N) (1)*	16. Doubt	*Sandeha Kariba (V) (3)* *Sandeha (N) (3)* *Sansaya (N) (3)* *Aasanka (N) (1)*
17. Sorrow	*Duukha Kariba (V) (1)* *Duukha (V) (7)* *Khyova (N) (1)*	17. Understand	*Bujhiba (V) (35)* *Upalabdhi Kariba (V) (3)* *Hrudayangama Kariba (V) (5)* *Matichhanna Heba (V) (1)* *Upalabdhi Heba (N) (5)*
18. Interest	*Aagrahi Heba (V) (1)* *Aagraha (N) (5)*	18. Decide	*Sthira Kariba (V) (3)* *Nirupana Kariba (V) (2)* *Nirupita (N) (3)* *Nirnaya (N) (1)*

(Contd...)

(Table 3.8d : Contd...)

19. Satisfaction	*Trupta Heba (V) (3)* *Santusta Heba (V) (3)* *Santosha (N) (1)* *Krutartha Heba (V) (1)*	19. Imagine	*Kalpana Kariba (V) (2)* *Kalpana (N) (8)* *Kalpita (N) (3)*
20. Afraid	*Bhaya Kariba (V) (3)* *Dariba (V) (1)* *Bhaya (N) (6)* *Aatankita (N) (1)*	20. Admit	*Sweekara Kariba (V) (9)* *Sweekar (N) (6)* *Sweekariya (N) (2)*
21. Excited	*Unnadana (N) (1)*	21. Confuse	*Baula Heba (V) (2)* *Bhramachhana Kariba (V) (1)* *Bhranta Kariba (V) (1)* *Bibhranta (N) (1)*
22. Pathos	*Karuna Kariba (V) (1)* *Karuna (V) (1)*	22. Confirm	*Sunischita (N) (10)*
23. Hesitate	*Niisankocha (N) (1)* *Kuntha (N) (2)*		

Table 3.9a : Lexical elaboration of metaperceptual and metalinguistic words and their frequencies in children's literature

Sl. No.	*Meta-perceptual Words*	*lexical Elaboration and Frequencies of Oriya words*	*Sl. No.*	*Meta linguistic*	*lexical Elaboration words Frequencies of and Oriya Words*
1.	Hear	*Suniba (V) (10)*	1.	Say	*Kahiba (V) (83)*
2.	See	*Dekhiba (V) (35)*			
		Chahinba (V) (3)			
		Anai (V) (3)			
		Lakhya Kariba (V) (1)	2.	Ask	*Pachariba (V) (5)*
			3.	Opinion	*Mata (N) (2)*
			4.	Remark	*Mantabya Deba (V) (2)*
			5.	Conversation	*Gapasapa Kariba (V) (2)*
			6.	Praise	*Prasansa Kariba (V) (10)*
			7.	Express	*Prakasa Kariba (V) (1)*

Table 3.9b: Lexical elaboration of metaperceptual and metalinguistic words and their frequencies in children's text books

Sl. No.	*Meta-perceptual Words*	*Lexical Elaboration and Frequencies of Oriya Words*	*Sl. No.*	*Meta-linguistic Words*	*Lexical Elaboration and Frequencies of Oriya Words*
1.	Hear	*Subhiba (V) (5)*	1.	Say	*Kahiba (V) (35)*
		Suniba (V) (6)			*Prakasa Kariba (V) (1)*
2.	See	*Dekhiba (V) (5)*	2.	Ask	*Pachariba (N) (1)*
			3.	Advice	*Upadesa (N) (1)*
			4.	Sympathy	*Samabedana (N) (1)*
			5.	Opinion	*Mata (N) (3)*
			6.	Discussion	*Aalochana Kariba (V) (1)*
			7.	Praise	*Prasansa Kariba (V) (8)*
			8.	Threaten	*Dhamaka Deba (V) (1)*
			9.	Explain	*Bujhaiba (V) (3)*

Table 3.9c : Lexical elaboration of metalinguistic and metaperceptual words and their frequencies in Oriya Novel

Sl. No.	*Meta-perceptual Words*	*Lexical Elaboration and frequencies of Oriya Words*	*Sl. No.*	*Meta-linguistic Words*	*Lexical Elaboration Frequencies of and Oriya Words*
1.	Say	*Kahiba (V) (276)*	1.	See	*Dekhiba (V) (70)*
		Janai Deba (V) (11)			*Anaiba (V) (5)*
		Prakasa Kariba (V) (1)			*Chahinba (V) (23)*
		Byakta Kariba (V) (1)			*Disiba (V) (7)*
		Swagatokti Kariba (V) (1)			*Adrusya Heba (V) (2)*
		Aabruti Kariba (V)(1)			*Darshana Kariba (V) (6)*
					Darshana (N) (3)
					Najara Padiba (V) (1)
					Prakata Heba (V) (1)
					Pradarsit Kariba (V) (1)
					Drusti Pakaiba (V) (2)

(Contd...)

(Table 3.9c : Contd....)

2. Ask	*Pachariba (V) (28)* *Bujhiba (V) (2)* *Jigyansa Kariba (V) (1)*	2. Hear	*Suniba (V) (24)*
3. Suggest	*Prastaba Deba (V) (3)* *Prastaba (N) (4)*	3. Notice	*Lakhya Kariba (V) (7)*
4. Declare	*Ghosana Kariba (V) (4)* *Prachara Kariba (V) (2)* *Praghata Kariba (V) (1)*	4. Search	*Thaba Kariba (V) (1)*
5. Blame	*Ninda Kariba (V) (2)* *Ninda (N) (2)*		
6. Complain	*Abhijoga (N) (3)* *Abhijukta Kariba (V) (1)*		
7. Question	*Prasnna Kariba (V) (5)* *Jera Kariba (V) (1)* *Prasnna (N) (7)*		
8. Order	*Aadesa (N) (9)* *Aadesa Kariba/Deba (V) (2)*		
9. Address	*Bhasana (N) (2)* *Udbodhana (N) (1)* *Sambhasana Kariba (V) (1)* *Sambodhana Kariba (V) (2)*		
10. Direct	*Nirddesa (N) (4)*		
11. Argue	*Jukta (N) (2)* *Tarka Kariba (V) (1)*		
12. Praise	*Prasansa (N) (4)* *Prasansa Kariba (V) (4)*		
13. Answer	*Uttara Deba (V) (17)* *Uttara (N) (9)*		
14. Remark	*Mantabya Deba /* *Kariba (V) (2)* *Mantabya (N) (1)* *Tippani (N) (2)* *Tippani Kariba (V) (1)*		
15. Describe	*Barnnana Kariba (V) (1)* *Bayana Kariba (V) (1)*		
16. Opinion	*Mata (N) (5)*		
17. Expression	*Bhaba (N) (1)* *Prakasa Kariba (V) (1)*		
18. Discuss	*Aalochana Kariba (V) (5)* *Aalochita Heba (V) (1)* *Aalochana (N) (2)*		
19. Mean	*Artha (N) (5)*		
20. Request	*Anurodha Kariba (V)(8)* *Anurodha (N) (6)*		
21. Advice	*Upadesa (N) (1)*		
22. Promise	*Pratignya Kariba (V) (2)* *Pratignya (N) (3)* *Sankalpa Kariba (V) (1)* *Pana Kariba (V) (2)*		
23. Explain	*Bujhaiba (V) (2)* *Kaiphiyat Chahinba (V) (1)*		

Table 3.9d : Lexical elaboration of metalinguistic and metaperceptual words and their frequencies in Oriya essay

Sl. No.	Meta-perceptual Words	Lexical Elaboration and Frequencies of Oriya Words	Sl. No.	Meta linguistic Words	Lexical Elaboration Frequencies of and Oriya Words
1.	Say	*Kahiba (V) (111)* *Sunaiba (V) (2)* *Boliba (V) (3)* *Boile (V)(2)* *Byakta Kariba (V) (2)*	1.	See	*Dekhiba (V) (74)* *Drustigochara Heba (V) (3)* *Paridrusta Deba (V) (2)* *Disiba (V) (20)* *Pratipadita Kariba (V) (1)* *Aneiba (V) (1)* *Chinhiba (V) (3)* *Najara (N) (1)* *Drusti (N) (5)* *Drusti Padiba/Heba (V) (2)* *Drusti Deba (V) (1)* *Drusti Rakhiba (V) (1)* *Darsana Kariba (V) (2)* *Drustipata Kariba (V) (1)* *Prakata Kariba (V) (1)*
2.	Ask	*Pachariba (V) (17)* *Bujhiba (V) (4)*	2.	Hear	*Suniba (V) (19)*
3.	Declare	*Ghosana Kariba (V) (8)* *Prachara Kariba (V) (2)*	3.	Notice	*Lakhya Kariba (V) (4)* *Parilakhita Heba (V) (3)*
4.	Blame	*Ninda Kariba (V) (1)*	4.	Observe	*Nirikhyana Kariba (V) (2)*
5.	Explain	*Bujhaiba (V) (4)* *Byakhya Kariba (V) (3)* *Byakhya (N) (2)*	5.	Search	*Khojiba (V) (1)* *Anusandhana Kariba (V) (1)* *Anusandhana (N) (2)* *Thaura Kariba (V) (1)*
6.	Question	*Prasna Kariba (V) (4)* *Prasna (N) (3)*	6.	Smell	*Aaghrana Kariba (V) (1)*
7.	Order	*Aadesa Kariba (V) (2)* *Aadesa (N) (4)*	7.	Sure	*Nischita Bhabare (V) (1)* *Nischaya (N) (7)*
8.	Directed	*Nirddesa Deba (V) (3)* *Nirddesita Kariba (V) (1)* *Nirddesa (V) (1)*	8.	Conclude	*Siddhantare-* *Pahanchhiba (V)(1)* *Siddhanta (N) (2)*
9.	Promise	*Sankalpa Kariba (V) (2)* *Pratignya (N) (2)* *Anurakta Rahiba (V) (1)* *Biswasa (V) (15)*	9.	Believe	*Biswasa Kariba (V) (5)*
10.	Praise	*Prasansa Kariba (V) (3)*	10.	Figure-out	*Dhariba/Dharineba/* *Dharaheba (V) (3)*
11.	Answer	*Uttara Deba (V) (5)* *Jabab Deba (V) (2)* *Kaifiyat Deba (V) (1)*	11.	Consciousness	*Chetanaa (N) (4)* *Prana (N) (1)*
12.	Argue	*Jukti (N) (3)* *Tarka (N) (1)*	12.	Dream	*Swapna (N) (1)*
13.	Request	*Anurodha Kariba (V) (1)*	13.	Discover	*Aabiskara Karithiba (V) (2)*
14.	Describe	*Barnnana Kariba (V) (5)* *Barnnita Thiba (V) (3)* *Barnnana (N) (1)* *Chitrana (N) (3)*	14.	Concentrate	*Dhhyana (N) (1)*
15.	Discuss	*Aalochana Kariba (V) (4)*	15.	Study	*Anudhhana (N) (2)*

(Contd...)

(Table 3.9d : Contd...)

	Aalochita Heba (V) (2) *Aalochana (N) (9)* *Aalokha (V) (1)* *Anusilana Kariba (V) (1)*		
16. Mention	*Ullekha Kariba (V) (4)* *Ullekhajogya (N) (3)*	16. Puzzling	*Rahasyamaya (N) (4)* *Mayaa (N) (1)*
17. Address	*Sambodhana Kariba (V) (4)* *Udbodhana (N) (1)* *Janaapadiba (V)(1)*	17. Appear	*Maneheba (V) (17)* *Pratiyaman Heba (V) (4)*
18. Opinion	*Mata (N) (7)*	18. Mind	*Mana (N) (2)* *Mane Mane (N) (3)* *Maanasika (N) (3)*
19. Mean	*Artha (N) (11)*	19. Compare	*Tulana Kariba (V) (1)* *Tulana (N) (4)*
20. Example	*Drustanta Deba (V) (1)* *Drustanta (N) (2)* *Udaharana (N) (3)*	20. Truth	*Satya (N) (6)*
21. Persuade	*Prabarttaiba (V) (1)*	21. Lie	*Mithya (N) (2)*
22. Advice	*Upadesa (N) (5)*	22. Intelligence	*Buddhi (N) (4)*
23. Expression	*Bhaba (N) (13)* *Bhaba Prakata Kariba (V) (1)*	23. Hesitate	*Dwanda (N) (2)3.* *Dwandare Padi (V) (1)*
24. Courage	*Sahasa Kariba (V) (2)* *Sahasa (N) (4)* *Sahasi (N) (2)*	24. Reading	*Padhiba (V) (6)*
25. Hate	*Ghruna (N) (2)*	25.. Conscience	*Bibeka (N) (7)*
26. Insult	*Tachhalya Kariba (V) (1)*		
27. Grateful	*Krutagnya Heba (V) (1)* *Krutagnyata (N) (3)*		
28. Console	*Aaswasta Heba/* *Kariba (V) (2)*		
29. Devotion	*Bhakti (N) (3)* *Anurakti (N) (2)* *Anuraga (N) (1)*		
30. Like	*Bhala Lagiba (V) (1)*		
31. Pride	*Garba Kariba (V) (2)* *Ahankara (N) (1)* *Ahamika (N) (1)* *Aatma Badima (N) (1)*		
32. Emotional	*Bhabaprabana (N) (2)*		
33. Attract	*Aakrusta Heba (V) (2)* *Aakarsana (N) (2)* *Chittakarsaka (N) (1)*		
34. Cruel	*Nrusansa (N) (1)*		
35. Affection	*Mamata (N) (2)*		
36. Indifferent	*Udasina Heba (V) (1)* *Bimukha Heba (V) (8)*		
37. Sympathy	*Darada (N) (1)* *Anukampaa (N) (1)* *Karuna (N) (1)* *Sahanubhuti (N) (1)*		
38. Frustration	*Hatasajanaka (N) (2)*		
39. Startle	*Chamki Padiba (V) (1)*		
40. Angry	*Ragijibaa (V) (1)* *Krodha (N) (1)* *Uttyakta Heba (V) (1)*		

(Contd...)

(**Table 3.9d** : Contd...)

41. Experience	Abhignyata (N) (2)
42. Joy	*Aananda Deba (V) (2)*
	Aananda (N) (8)
	Ullasita Heba (V) (1)
	Upabhoga Kariba (V) (1)
	Aahllada (N) (1)
43. Anxiety	*Nirudbega (N) (1)*
44. Confuse	*Bichalita Heba (V) (1)*
45. Peace	*Shanti (N) (5)*
46. Calm	*Shanti Heba (V) (5)*

The Field Study

A brief summary of the result obtained from the field research is given below followed by a detailed discussion.

(1) Frequency of occurrence is more among literate adults than semiliterate and illiterate adults. Similarly frequency of occurrence is more among schooled children than among unschooled children.
(2) The most frequently occurred words are metalinguistic followed by metacognitive, meta-affective and metaperceptual words among the adults as well as children irrespective of variation in literacy.
(3) Varied use of mental state words is not observed among semiliterate adults, illiterate adults and unschooled children.

Metacognitive Words

Consideration of the list of metacognitive words (Tables 3.10, 3.14, 3.15) shows that the varieties of words and their frequencies are more in literate adults and schooled children than in semiliterate, illiterate and unschooled children. Frequencies of metacognitive words are more in semiliterate adults compared to illiterate adults. Literate adults and schooled children use the words: 'remember', 'know', 'understand' and 'sure' more frequently compared to semiliterate, illiterate and unschooled children. Frequency of occurrence of cognitive words like 'think', 'know', 'sure' and 'understand' have occurred maximally in literate adults than semiliterate and illiterate adults.

But in case of unschooled children 'think' is the only metacognitive word that has occurred most frequently compared to the schooled children. There are some cognitive words (such as: believe and learn) that had not occurred at all among literate adults compared to semiliterate and illiterate adults.

Table 3.10. Lexical elaboration of metacognitive words and their frequencies in oral conversation among literate, semiliterate, and illiterate adults

Sl. No.	Meta-cognitive Words	Literate	Semi-literate	Illiterate
1.	Think	*Bhabiba (V) (60)* *Chinta Kariba (V) (13)*	*Bhabiba (V) (25)* *Chinta Kariba (V) (4)*	*Bhabiba (V) (19)* *Chinta Kariba (V) (4)*
2.	Know	*Janiba (V) (27)*	*Janiba (V) (8)*	*Janiba (V) (22)*
3.	Understand	*Bujhiba (V)(31)*	*Bujhiba (V) (13)*	*Bujhiba (V) (17)*
4.	Mind	*Mana (V) (4)*	*Mana (V) (7)*	*Mana (V) (5)*
5.	Sure	*Nischaya (V) (24)*	*Nischaya (V) (3)*	*Nischaya (V) (2)*
6.	Lie	*Mithya (V) (1)*	–	–
7.	Remember	*Mane Rahiba (V) (3)* *Mane Padiba (V) (3)*	–	– *Mane Pakaiba (V) (1)*
8.	Effort	*Chesta (V) (2)*	–	–
9.	Forget	*Bhulijiba (V) (2)*	–	–
10.	Believe	–	*Biswas (V) (1)*	*Biswas (V) (2)*
11.	Learn	–	*Sikhiba (V) (2)*	–

Meta-affective Words

Tables 3.11, 3.14, 3.15 shows the frequency of occurrence and the varieties of meta-affective words among adults in three literacy levels and 8, 10 and 12 year old schooled and unschooled children.

The frequency of occurrence and varieties of meta-affective words are more in literate adults and schooled children compared to the other two literacy levels and unschooled children. The occurrence of meta-affective words is more in illiterate adults than in semiliterate adults. The most frequently occurred meta-affective words among literate adults compared to semiliterate and illiterate adults are: desire, like, worry, fear, and disgust. Where as 'sorrow' and 'happy' have occurred maximally in illiterate adults than in literate adults. There are some words (such as: love, satisfaction and hate) which have not occurred in the discource of literate adults compared to semiliterate and illiterate adults. Table 3.14 shows that 'desire' is the only meta-affective word that occurred more frequently in schooled children than in unschooled children. There are some meta-affective words such as 'worry', 'fear' and 'like', that had not occurred in the discourse of the schooled children compared to the unschooled children.

Table 3.11. Lexical elaboration of metaffective words and their frequencies in oral conversation of literate, semi-literate and illiterate adults

Sl. No.	*Meta-cognitive Words*	*Literate*	*Semi-literate*	*Illiterate*
1.	Desire	*Echha (V) (33)*	*Echha (V) (10)* *Echha (V) (15)*	*Chahein (V) (1)* *Mana Baleiba (V) (1)*
2.	Sorrow	*Duukha Kariba (V) (5)*	*Duukha Kariba (V) (15)*	*Duukha Kariba (V) (17)*
3.	Happy	*Khusi (V) (6)* *Thatta/Majja (V) (1)*	*Khusi (V) (6)*	*Khusi (V) (6)* *Sukha (V) (1)*
4.	Like	*Bhala Lagiba (V) (18)* *Pasanda Kariba (V) (2)*	*Bhala Lagiba (V) (4)*	*Bhala Lagiba (V) (4)*
5.	Pain	*Kasta (V) (16)*	*Kasta (V) (18)*	*Kasta (V) (13)*
6.	Worry	*Byasta (V) (13)*	–	*Byasta (V) (2)*
7.	Fear	*Dara (V) (15)*	*Dara (V) (1)*	*Dara (V) (4)*
8.	Disgust	*Birakta (V)(6)*	–	*Birakta (V)(1)*
9.	Expectation	*Aasaa (V) (1)*	*Aasaa (V) (1)*	–
10.	Anger	*Ragiba (V) (1)*	–	–
11.	Love	–	*Bhala Paiba (V) (4)*	*Bhala Paiba (V) (1)*
12.	Satisfaction	–	*Trupti (V) (3)*	–
13.	Hate	–		*Ghruna (V) (1)*

Metaperceptual Words

Literate adults and schooled children showed higher frequencies of metaperceptual words compared to semiliterate, illiterate adults and unschooled children. The frequency of occurrence is more in illiterate adults than semiliterate adults. Literate adults and schooled children use the words 'see' and 'hear' more frequently compared to semi-literate, illiterate adults and unschooled children (Tables 3.12, 3.14 and 3.15).

Table 3.12 : Lexical elaboration of meta-perceptual words and their frequencies in oral conversation among literate, semi-literate and illiterate adults

Sl. No.	*Meta-cognitive words*	*Literate*	*Semi-literate*	*Illiterate*
1.	See	*Dekhiba (V) (81)* *Chahinba (V) (3)*	*Dekhiba (V) (14)* *Chahinba (V) (3)*	*Dekhiba (V) (43)* *Najar Pakaiba (V) (27)*
2.	Hear	*Suniba (V) (17)*	*Suniba (V) (1)*	*Suniba (V) (16)*
3.	Search	*Khojiba (V) (2)*	–	*Khojiba (V) (2)*

Metalinguistic Words

Tables 3.13, 3.14, 3.15 show that the frequency of occurrence of metalinguistic word is more in literate adults and schooled children than in semiliterate, and illiterate adults and unschooled children. The occurrence of metalinguistic words is more in semiliterate adults compared to illiterate adults. These tables also show that only two words that occurred frequently among adults and children are 'say' and 'ask'. The word 'say' is the only metalinguistic word that has occurred maximally among adults and children. Table 3.13 shows that literate adults use the word 'say' more frequently compared to semiliterate and illiterate adults. Similarly, schooled children use the word 'say' more frequently compared to unschooled children. However, literate adults use the word 'say' more frequently than the schooled children.

Table 3.13: Lexical elaboration of meta-linguistic words and their frequencies in oral conversation among literate, semi-literate and illiterate adults

Sl. No.	*Meta-cognitive Words*	*Literate*	*Semi-literate*	*Illiterate*
1.	Say	*Kahiba (V) (183)*	*Kahiba (V) (31)*	*Kahiba (V) (97)*
2.	Ask	*Pachariba (V) (5)*	*Pachariba (V) (1)*	*Pachariba (V) (2)*

Table 3.14: Lexical elaboration of meta-cognitive, metalinguistic, meta-affective and metaperceptual words in oral conversation of schooled children from 8yrs., 10yrs., and12yrs, age group

Sl No.	*Meta-cognitive Words*	*Lexical Elaboration and Frequencies*	*Sl. No.*	*Meta-cognitive Words*	*Lexical Elaboration and Frequencies*
1.	Think	*Bhabiba (V) (18)* *Chinta Kariba (V) (5)*	1.	Say	*Kahiba (V) (147)*
2.	Know	*Janiba (V) (22)*	2.	Ask	*Pachariba (V) (6)*
3.	Understand	*Bujhiba (V) (24)*			
4.	Sure	*Nischaya (V) (19)*			
5.	Believe	*Biswas Kariba (V) (2)*			
6.	Remember	*Mane Rahiba (V) (12)*			
7.	Mind	*Mana (V) (9)*			
8.	Conscience	*Bibeka (V) (1)*			

Sl. No.	*Meta-affective Words*	*Lexical Elaboration and Frequencies*	*Sl. No.*	*Meta-perceptual Words*	*Lexical Elaboration and Frequencies*
1.	Desire	*Echha Kariba (V) (21)*	1.	See	*Dekhiba (V) (68)* *Chahinba (V) (1)*
2.	Sorrow	*Duukha (V) (6)* *Mana Kharap (V) (6)*	2.	Hear	*Suniba*
3.	Happy	*Khusi Heba (V) (7)*	3.	Search	*Khojiba (V) (2)*
4.	Love	*Bhal Paiba (V) (2)*			
5.	Pain	*Kasta (V) (15)*			
6.	Frustrated	*Hatas Heba (V) (4)*			
7.	Satisfaction	*Santusta (V) (4)*			
8.	Expectation	*Aasakariba (V) (1)*			
9.	Disgust	*Birakta (V) (8)*			
10.	Afraid	*Dara (V) (15)*			
11.	Affection	*Mamata (V) (1)*			

Table 3.15 : Lexical elaboration of meta-cognitive, metalinguistic, meta-affective and metaperceptual words in oral conversation of unschooled children from 8yrs.,10yrs., and 12yrs., age group.

Sl. No.	*Meta-cognitive Words*	*Lexical Elaboration and Frequencies*	*Sl. No.*	*Meta-cognitive Words*	*Lexical Elaboration and Frequencies*
1.	Think	*Bhabiba (V) (25)* *Chinta Kariba (V) (4)*	1.	Say	*Kahiba (V) (33)*
2.	Mind	*Mana (V) (2)*	2.	Ask	*Pachariba (V) (1)*
3.	Know	*Janiba (V) (9)*			
4.	Sure	*Nischaya (V) (3)*			
5.	Remember	*Mane Padiba (V) (1)*			

Sl. No.	*Meta-affective Words*	*Lexical Elaboration and frequencies*	*Sl. No.*	*Meta-perceptual Words*	*Lexical Elaboration and Frequencies*
1.	Desire	*Eccha (V) (10)*	1.	Hear	*Suniba (V) (4)*
2.	Happy	*Khusi (V) (5)*	2.	See	*Dekhiba (V) (13)* *Chahinba (V) (4)*
3.	Sorrow	*Duukha Kariba (V)(15)*			
4.	Love	*Bhal pae (V) (2)*			
5.	Like	*Bhala Lage (V) (1)*			
6.	Pain	*Kasta (V) (15)*			
7.	Worry	*Byasta (V) (1)*			
8.	Fear	*Dara (V) (5)*			

The comparison of the existence and use of mental state words among adults has interesting implications for language development. Even though in Oriya language there is varied lexical elaboration of mental state vocabulary, adults rarely use them in their oral conversation. It would be interesting to observe how children learn mental state words in this language with minimal exposure to such language in adult conversation.

Chapter-4

Development of Mental State Vocabulary

The young child's acquisition of mental state words has attracted interest for a number of reasons. First, as part of the early lexicon of children, mental terms are of interest in their own right. Second as discussed earlier, the acquisition of mental terms may be taken as indicating an understanding of mental state and therefore, reflects the development of the concept of mind in children (Johnson, 1982). The importance of mental state verbs in children's lexicon would be discussed in detail later.

The acquisition process of mental state words can be divided into two stages: (1) Early acquisition of basic words, such as: know, think, say, etc. and (2) a stage of further elaboration of the basic words. Most of the research done on early acquisition stage revealed that some mental terms, such as know, think, and remember start to appear in children's lexicon in the second and third year of life (Bretherton & Beeghly, 1982; Shatz, Wellman & Silber, 1983) and complete understanding of the semantic and pragmatic properties of such mental state words in English occur around 4 to 5 years of age (Moore, Bryant, & Furrow 1989; Moore & Davidge, 1989; Moore, Harris & Patriquin, 1993). Studies done on early acquisition of metarepresentational verbs in Oriya language has revealed that words such as say, know, think, sad/happy acquired by children between two to five years of age (Satpathy, 1993; Babu & Mishra, 2000). The existence of such words in Oriya speaking literate, illiterate and oral literate adults is evident from the study conducted by Babu and Mamata (1992). Further elaborations of basic terms like say, think, know is evident in a study by Astington and Olson (1986). They reported that a significant development of mental state terms to replace simple verbs like 'say' and 'think' occur by 10 to 19 years and onwards. Similar finding has been obtained by Mishra (1994) in a study on further elaboration of the mental state words (say and think) in Oriya language.

During 3 to 4 years of age children acquire the lexical terms for a set of mental concepts including know, think, remember, forget, dream, pretend etc. They talk about desires and emotions before they talk about beliefs. The first desire term children use is 'want'. In Bartsch and Wellman (1995) study this term comprised 97 per cent of all desire expressions in the data. Bartsch and Wellman also identified times when the child made an explicit contrast between his or her own psychological state and that of another person. Even two year olds can make explicit distinction between their own and other's desires. Two years old also talk about feelings, again, both of their own and those of other people. This vocabulary increases remarkably during their third year (Ridgeway, Waters & Kuczaj, 1985). Most two year olds know words for the six universal basic emotions — happiness, sadness, fear, anger, surprise and disgust (Bretherton & Beeghly 1982; Babu & Rath, 2002). From $2^1/_2$ years on, children use mental terms such as think, know and remember in their spontaneous speech (Limber, 1973). The occurrence of such lexical items might be taken as evidence that children have a theory of mind. (Bretherton, McNew & Beeghly, 1981). They claim that mental terms are applied to oneself before they are applied to others.

The general finding, from Bretherton, Dunn, Wellman and others is that children have terms for perception, emotion and desire in their vocabulary before they use words to refer to cognitive states. The first belief terms children use are 'think' and 'know'. These two words comprised 94 per cent of all the belief expressions in Bartsch and Wellman's study (1995). These words are commonly used by the end of third year of life.

The above discussed developmental research on children's understanding of mental verbs like want, think, know etc. have focused on observation of appearance of these words in the productive lexicons of young children. Developmental research in this area has also focused on another related property of these terms: their presuppositions and implications.

Wellman and Estes (1987) attempted to describe the functions of these terms in young children's speech. They distinguished instances of genuine reference to the mind, the psychological use of these terms — from mere conversational or uninterpretable uses (Wellman, 1991). They concluded that the earliest uses of mental terms tend to be 'conversational' and not for true mental state reference. For example, a child may use the term 'know' in saying, "know what?" to introduce a new topic, a conversational use, in contrast to psychological use, which actually refers to someone's knowing in "I did not know you had this". This is discussed in the previous chapter. Wellman (1991) opines that although two year olds may use the words 'think' and 'know', they do not use these terms for psychological reference or do so only rarely just before the third birthday. The use of 'think' and 'know', for psychological reference increase remarkably during the fourth year. By four years of age children can explicitly contrast their own beliefs with those of another.

If the child's language is to be taken as a measure of the mental life understanding, mere production of particular words cannot be taken as its index. As already discussed those utterances may or may not refer to mental states, but may be used for conversational purposes. It is essential, therefore, to go beyond and obtain assessment of the semantic and pragmatic functions of those words referring to mental states. The second approach to the study of the development of mental terms has been to examine experimentally the understanding of the semantic distinctions underlying the words and pragmatic use of these words.

Many experimental studies have investigated semantic distinctions of these words using negation test, where (Macnamara, Baker & Olson, 1976; Scoville & Gordon, 1980; Abbeduto & Rosenberg, 1985) children are required to comment on the truth-value of statements taken from either factive or non-factive contexts.

Presupposition is also used to refer to the beliefs of the subject of the sentence using mental verb. According to this kind of analysis, a term such as 'know' can be differentiated from one such as think in that the former implies that the subject of the verb has an unambiguous evidence, either perceptual or inferential as to the truth of the complement, while the latter implies that the subject does not have such evidence. The technique has been to request the children to select the mental term that best describes a person's mental orientation towards a particular statement or event. The correct choice is supposed to reflect the understanding that the different terms require different evidential bases. Studies have been done by Johnson and Maratsos (1977); Miscione, Marvin, O'Brien and Greenberg (1978); Wellman and Johnson (1979); Johnson and Wellman (1980); Abbeduto and Rosenberg, (1985), Babu (1989), Babu & Mishra (2000) in this regard.

The consensus from most of the studies seems to be that children do not start to differentiate the verbs on the basis of their presuppositions until four to five years of age.

Study conducted in India by Babu & Mishra (2000) using the tasks of presupposition has revealed that among Oriya speaking children the semantic properties of 'think' and 'know' is a latter development than the English speaking children and the complete understanding of mental state words is not achieved by 7 years of age.

As understanding of the semantics is only one aspect of the acquisition of mental or indeed any terms. It is also important for children to recognize how they are used pragmatically. Although this issue has been raised in the literature (Johnson & Wellman, 1980; Shaz *et al*, 1983), it had not until recently been studied experimentally. A common function of mental verbs is to mark the degree of certainty, with which a statement is made (Urmson, 1963; Richards, 1982) for example, the speaker of the sentence — 'I know the boy is playing outside' — expresses more certainty that the boy is playing outside than does the speaker of the sentence— ' I think the boy is playing outside'.

In a study, Moore, Bryant and Furrow (1989) designed a task to investigate, whether children understand the use of mental terms to express differential degrees of certainty; a function that Shatz *et al.* (1983) lableded as 'modulation of assertion'. The task required children to find a hidden object, on the basis of statements, made by two speakers, varying in degree of certainty. They found that the ability to distinguish the degree of certainty expressed by the word 'know' from that expressed by 'think' and 'guess' developed from three to five years of age. 'Think' was not distinguished from 'guess' at any age up to eight years in the study. Moore and Davidge (1989) examined whether children's understanding of the expression of certainty might be distinguished from their understanding of the factive-non-factive distinction. The study revealed that children's understanding of the use of 'be sure' to express certainty developed along with their understanding of 'know' and 'think' between 4 to 5 years of age.

The finding of a parallel development for the understanding of factivity and certainty expression in experimental tasks raises the question of the relationship between the semantic and pragmatic aspects of these mental terms. It has been implied (Shatz, *et al.*, 1983) that the use of mental terms to express degrees of certainty is based on the factive-non-factive properties of these terms, and for this function, therefore, that pragmatics depend upon semantics. On the other hand, it is equally possible to take the opposite position, that factivity is best understood in terms of pragmatics.

Bartsch and Wellman (1995) had suggested three stages in development of children's talk about the mind. There is an early phase when children talk about desires, essentially wants and likes, in a wide variety of situations: desires for objects, actions, current or future states of affairs and their own desires and the desires of others.This early talk about desires is followed by a second phase, often beginning about the third birthday, in which children begin to talk about beliefs and thoughts as well as desires. In the second phase, from about 3 to 4 years of age, children talk about desires much more often than thoughts and beliefs, and although they are willing to describe people as having beliefs their explanations for actions appeal to desires.

In the third phase (which begins around 4 years), children grant the constructs of thoughts and beliefs a larger role in their basic understanding of mind and action. They increasingly refer to thoughts and beliefs and, moreover, they appeal to persons,' beliefs as true or false, in order to explain their actions. Investigators have been prepared to believe that talking and thinking about the mind is frequent in even young children. Furrow *et al.* (1992) recorded two-hour language samples from 19 children at age 2; 0 and again at 3; 0. They followed the methods of Shatz *et al.* (1983) to code genuine reference to thoughts and beliefs. Furrow *et al.* did not examine reference to desires and because of their small speech sample, were also unable to examine more intensively children's conceptions in such utterances as contrastives. However, they do report that references to thoughts and beliefs were essentially absent at 2; 0 but quite apparent in the same children sampled at age 3. More recently, Moore, Furrow, Chiasson, and Patriquin (1993) presented tallies of belief and desire terms (Simple use of the terms, not coded for psychological reference) for the same children. They report frequent use of desire terms (206 uses for the 19 children) at age 2 when there was very little use of belief or thought terms (35 total uses). The study reported later among oriya speaking children demonstrates the developmental milestones in the appearance of mental state words in the vocabulary of these children.

Relevant Research Issues

At this point two major questions can be raised. They are:

(1) First, would there be any variation in acquisition of mental state words among children exposed to different literacy environment? Till date, a number of researches has shown that the general language development of a child is influenced by the literacy environment in which the child is reared, such as family background, parent-child interaction pattern etc. The literate parents interact with

their children in a way which facilitates the development of a more sophisticated language in their children compared to that of the children of illiterate parents. The study by Furrow, Moore, Davidge & Chiasson (1992) suggests the possibility that the development of mental state language and a theory of mind is fostered by the tendency of mothers to focus their children's attention on mental processes by talking about such processes, and more importantly by using utterances which conveniently direct the children to reflect on their own mental states. Besides, parent-child interaction, schooling may also facilitate the acquisition of metarepresentational words. Probably no other institute has so much opportunity as the school to shape the developing child. The schooled children are in a better position to acquire the metarepresentational words, because of their frequent use in the textbooks, in classroom interaction and peer-group interaction compared to that of their unschooled counterpart. Thus, it is expected that there would be difference in acquisition of meta-representational words on the basis of the type of literacy environment to which children are exposed. The next section would discuss this question in the context of acquisition of metarepresentational language among Oriya speaking children.

(2) The second but the most important question is: why do we need mental state terms in our vocabulary? Such terms are important for a number of reasons: Firstly, from a developmental perspective one need to learn these terms to refer to others mental states. For example, one can say, "I think it will rain" or equivalently, "it might rain", or "possibly it will rain". The mental verb "think", verb modal "might" and adverb "possibly" marks uncertainty of the propositions from his own point of view. However, if one wants to refer to another person's uncertain mental state, he cannot use "verb modal" or "adverb" alone, he has to

use the mental state verbs "think". Thus, mastery of these terms is required for a proper adaptation in social interation.

Secondly, it is needed in a literate culture because: (a) for increased precision in technical discourse, one needs to differentiate between uncertainty (think, guess) and certainty (know), or differentiate between different levels of processes like recall and recognition, (b) to permit lexicalisation in written language of the extra and paralinguistic features of spoken language, for example, "I insist . . . . . . " replacing an insistent tone.

Thirdly, to develop an awareness and mastery on one's knowledge state, one needs to have elaborated and differentiated terms for thought and talk. Papert (1980) pointed out that "the ability to articulate the processes of thinking enables us to improve them". Thus the vocabulary in the internal state domain determines to a large extent the repertoire of concepts in this area and ones reflection or awareness of these concepts. Therefore, one would expect that certain mental state word usage would correlate with skill in metacognitive processes; and will also correlate with greater readiness for and success in school. Metacognition, whether in the broader or narrower sense, clearly cannot be equated with the use of mental state words. However, it is true that every meaningful use of a mental state word does indicate an act of metacognition on the part of the speaker. There is some evidence that children's knowledge of the structure of language, part of the metalanguage is important in learning to read. Reid (1966), Downing and Leong (1982), Wells (1985) and others have shown that children's knowledge of the metalinguistic nouns, sentences, words, letters, and sound is important in learning to read and write an alphabetic word based script. Olson and Torrance (1983) argued that the thoughts a child or an adult can think are closely related to the utterances the child or adult can generate and/or comprehend. And one important means of examining children's thought and language is via their knowledge of the corresponding verbs of saying and meaning.

The Role of Socio-cultural Variables on the Acquisition of Mental State Language and Theory of Mind

Human development is to be understood in the context of the social system and interpersonal relations (Vygotsky, 1978). The social system itself is a product of a history of cultural evolution. As such, individuals are historically situated and their thought processes are mediated by a variety of cultural tools, which are products of a long process of development of cultures. For Vygotsky (1978) language is the most fundamental of all the cultural tools, which mediate our higher mental functions. At the same time language is also learned through social interaction. Thus, language is both a tool and a product of social processes. Several studies confirm Vygotsky's (1978) claim regarding the role of social interactions in cognition. Ochs (1986) and Gardner (1984), for example, documented how children's competence in the use of language for communication and other social functions was shaped through their participations in social interaction with adults. Through such interactions, adults provided necessary "Scaffolding" (Bruner, 1975, 1978) by structuring the communicative acts to facilitate development of children's linguistic competence children's acquisition of knowledge is basically a social process influenced by all levels of social interaction with adults as well as children (Babu & Mohanty, 2001). In particular, the cooperative task of conversation enables the child to internalize ways of thinking through exposure to conversation about "thinking" with adult partners (Astington, 1996; Symons, 2004). Brownwell and Carriger (1991) demonstrated that quite early in development (i.e. less than 3 years) children are influenced by peer social contexts. Vygotsky (1967) suggested that play; including pretend play, creates a zone of proximal development for the child. Zone of proximal development is viewed as the distance between a child's actual developmental level and the higher level of potential development as determined through adult guidance or peer collaboration. Participation in pretend play situations helps children to understand that representations are different from reality and also that representations are not always socially shared. The above discussion thus raised a number of questions regarding the universality *versus* culture specificity of developing a theory of mind.

Cross-cultural Variation in Acquisition of Mental State Understanding

Avis & Harris (1991) have recently shown that Baka children of Cameroon develop the ability to predict action and emotion based on person's belief and desire at roughly the same age that western children do. On the other hand McCormicks, (1990) recent data has shown that 4 years to 7 years old Quecha children of Peru, whose language has a well developed vocabulary for appearance reality but not for belief, do well on appearance reality but fail on false belief task using the same materials.

Parent-Child Interaction and Child's Development of Mental State Language

As already discussed, culture mediates its impact through social interactions between children and their parents, peer-group, neighbours, grandparents, etc. Parents are the most important agent of the society and in the life of the child. Psychological research and current popular writing have suggested that the amount of time children spend in activities with parents contribute significantly to children's development of behaviour in general, and to cognitive development and academic achievement in particular. Children's talk, in their early years is generally acquired and developed in the home. The environment that parents provide for these children is the one their children learn from. It can help or hinder their ability to be active participants in their own learning. It can provide rich or impoverished contents. Parental input has been shown to relate closely to the order of acquisition of general vocabulary items (Huttenlocher, Haight, Bryk, Seltzer & Lyons, 1991).

Not all children learn in the same way or at the same rate but there seems to be consistent pattern of interaction, which correlates with children's ability to enjoy and benefit from the literate environment of home. Parents, who talk to their children, show sensitivity to their children's ability and also draw them on the more and more complex behaviours. Children then are more able to be masters of their own progress supported by these affective and cognitive stimulating interactions. Parents and other adults use a variety of devices that aid the child learning of metalanguage. During the course of their normal social interaction parents often introduce objects to provide a basis for their mutual play and speak about object and events that are present and easily visible to the child. Parents do other helpful things as well. They closely monitor their child's apparent goals and intentions during most of their interactive turns; they attempt to modulate, correct or elaborate their child's behaviour rather than redirect it. And they construct an internal model of their child's current preferences, skills, and world knowledge, which they continuously updates and check (Fischer & Bullock, 1984). These strategies make comprehension easier for children. However, the tactics that parents use are usually not deliberate teaching techniques; instead, they follow naturally from simply trying to carry on conversation with a child.

Several researches emphasized the role of parents as educators (Lamb & Lamb,1978; Lille & Forhanis, 1976; Arnold, 1978; Morrison, 1978; Fine, 1980; Abidin,1980 and Berger,1981). Blackstone (1979), Pugh (1981) & Pugh & De'Ath (1984) have all made notable contributions to the notion of parent-child discourse as a facilitator of the child's language development. Shukla (1988) demonstrated the role of mothers in shaping their children's style and functional priorities in the use of language. Babu (2005) observed that parent-child interaction particularly the use of some strategies such as questioning, initiation and help in doing a task; corrections are significantly related to metaliguistic skills and emergent reading of the children. Children do not have clear notions about the ability of reading or fully comprehend the basic terminology used in the course of instruction. Terms such as sound, word, space etc. are used by adults to facilitate children's understanding of metalinguistic terms.

Studies related to parent child contact in socially disadvantaged homes indicate that children's language superiority is attributed to opportunities for conversation with parents. Berko-Gleasen (1973) viewed that parental sensitivity of children's abilities is an important factor in determining how parents interact with their children linguistically and other areas of their lives as well. Gottfried & Gottfried (1984) found from their studies that higher secondary children had more books had more conversation during meal time with parents and received less harsh punishment. So far the discussion is restricted to the impact of parent-child interaction in overall language and literacy development. The following section deals with parent-child interaction and development of theory of mind and mental state language.

Johnson (1991) considers the role of social experience, particularly the role of parental talk, in transforming children's pre-reflective experience of mental states into reflective understanding of them. For example, young children are often frustrated by the conflict they experience between their own desires and intentions and those of others; parents may try to defuse such conflict by explaining it to the child using mental state terminology: "He didn't know you wanted it, and so on." The simulation theorists viewed concepts originating from introspections though it is not clear how children come to think of their own mental states in terms of beliefs and desires. An alternative view is that enculturation is itself the source of child's mental state understanding. Bruner (1983, 1990) wrote that parent treat infant's spontaneous gestures as intentional communications and thus infants come to see themselves as having intentions and start to communicate intentionally. In a similar way, parent's talk to todllers about their thoughts, feelings, and desires, and the children come to see themselves as holding such states. Parents also use the same linguistic terms to talk about other people.

Researchers (Dunn, Bretherton, & Munn, 1987; Nelson, Plesa & Henseler, 1998) have utilized a social constructive account to explain how children develop ToM concepts. According to this view, children's reasoning about the mind is advanced through participation in a type of interpretive narrative discourse. Through enculturation in social contexts, children learn to assign meaning to what people do, feel, and think. At the same time, they develop the ability to tell stories about themselves and other people, providing them a vehicle for integrating the thoughts, feelings, and actions of themselves and others. The emhasis is upon the conversational discourse in the family.

In everyday language directed at 16-month-old, caregiver use desired terms (specifically "want") were much more frequent than other internal state terms and references to "think" and "know" increased with age (Beeghly, Bretherton, & Mervis, 1986; Ruffman *et al.*, 2002) although the proportion of desire terms to think and know terms may vary considerably for individual children (Bartsch & Wellman, 1995). References to pleasure and distress are the most frequently occurring emotion terms (Brown & Dunn, 1991; Dunn *et al.* 1987; 1991). Thus before two years parents seem to refer to most children's desires and emotions.

Meins *et al.* (2003) examined maternal language directed to babies. They found that mothers' "appropriate" (i.e., comments that accurately reflected the child's mental states) but not in appropriate mind minded comments to 6-month-olds predicted child performance on a false belief task at 45-48 months of age. Ruffman *et al.* (2002) specifically compared mother mental state language with non-mental state language. They found that it was only mental state language—mothers use of "think" and "know" modulations of assertion, and desire term used with 3-4-year-old children that predicted later success on theory of mind tasks and children's mental state talk. Later research further confirmed the findings that maternal talk significantly relates to desire language and emotion understanding in children (Taumoepeau & Ruffman, 2006).

Perner (1988) found that children from large families are more likely to perform successfully on false belief tasks. They have explained that this may be so, because of their parent's explanation of these interactions, talk about who know this, who knew that and who wants that and so on. Brown and Dunn (1991) and Dunn (1988) showed that children who heard more talk about feeling and participated in family conversations at 18 months of age talked about feelings and understand different emotions and other people's experiences of emotion as well as their own. Further Dunn, Brown and Beardsall (1991) and Moore *et al.* (1994) have shown that children' whose mothers used more words like 'know' and 'think' when children were 2 years old were themselves more likely to use there words at 4 years of age in their talk and performed better in a test of their understanding of the distinction between 'knowing' and 'thinking'. Mishra (1994) in her study concluded that family and social interaction play a more important role than text books in the development of metarepresentational language. In families children listen to stories in which mentalistic talk is emphasised and they retell such states in their stories as well (Babu, 1989). These experiences are essential for child's acquisition of metarepresentational language. Presence of sibling also facilitates children's acquisition of theory of mind, more specifically their explanations involving reference to the others mental states (Das & Babu, 2004).

Furrow, Moore, Davidge and Chiasson (1992), have speculated the potential role of environment in the development and use of mental terms. Their result showed that the use of mental terms by children is strongly related to that by their mothers. Most importantly, mother's total use of mental term utterances when their children were 2, was significantly correlated with their children's use at 3. This relationship raised the possibility that growth in children's use of mental state terms was depended on their mother's use of such terms. Dunn *et al.* (1991) in the study reported earlier concluded that children's development of a theory of mind in mediated by talk and interactions within the family.

Thus, the development of mental state language is fostered by talking about such processes during family conversations and more importantly by using utterances which conceivably direct the children to reflect on their own mental states. The following studies intend at investigating some of the research issues discussed above among Oriya speaking children and adolescents.

Development of Mental State Words during Early Childhood: A Study among Oriya Speaking Children

The research was undertaken to investigate the acquisition of mental state words among 2- to- 3-years' old Oriya children, from Orissa, India. Further the role of parent literacy on acquisition of such words and the relationship between developing theory of mind and child's language and literacy acquisition was also investigated. The data was collected by a longitudinal as well as a cross-sectional method. Following longitudinal approach twenty-three 2-year-old children were studied for a period of 1 year to investigate their acquisition of a period of mental state words. These children were taken from 3 levels of parent literacy: Literate, semi-literate and illiterate parent with 10, 7 and 6 children respectively from each group. Parent-child interaction on different occasions like story-telling time, meal-time, sleep time, play-time etc. was recorded and later transcribed. The frequency of occurrence of mental state words in child's speech over 1 year period was noted to find out the development of such words among children from 2- to- 3- and half years of age. Parent conversations were also analysed.

Following cross sectional approach the research was carried out with a 2 (age) × 3 (literacy level) factorial design. There were two age groups of children: 3 years and 4 years from literate, semiliterate and illiterate parent groups. There were 75 children in each of the two age groups. Out of 75 children 25 children were taken from each parent literacy level. In order to study the relationship between developing a theory of mind child's acquisition of language and literacy skills a number of tasks were administered to the children such as:

(1) Appearance-Reality task,
(2) False-Belief task,
(3) See-Know task (Measuring Origin of Knowledge),
(4) Metalinguistic task, and
(5) Emergent Reading Skills.

Participants

In the longitudinal study, twenty-three 2-year-old Oriya speaking children were studied for 1 year. These children were taken from 3 levels of parent literacy such as: literate, semi-literate and illiterate with 10, 7 and 6 children respectively from each group.

In the cross-sectional study, a group of Oriya children from the age group of 3 years and 4 years were taken from three different parent literacy levels such as: Literate, semi-literate and illiterate. Seventy-five children from each of the two age groups from the different parent literacy level were taken randomly from pre-schools and Anganwadies in Orissa, India. The total sample, therefore, is 150 over all age levels and literacy levels. Other confounding variables like mother tongue, SES, area of residence, medium of instruction was controlled as far as possible.

Method of Observation

(a) Longitudinal Study

Twenty-three 2-year-old children were longitudinally studied for 1 year to investigate their acquisition of mental state words. These children were taken from 3 levels of literacy: Literate parent, semi-literate and illiterate parent with 10, 7 and 6 children respectively from each group. Parent child interaction on different occasions like dinner-time, play-time, story-telling time etc. was recorded by using voice activated tape recorder. Such recordings were made twice a month. Recorded conversation was transcribed and analysed later. This procedure also allowed us to detect the quality of parent child interaction and parent literacy on acquisition of internal state or mental state words. The literacy level of the parent was determined by an assessment of reading and writing skills. The literacy environment at home was studied by an informal home assessment scale. The frequency of occurrence of mental state words at different age level was analysed and a milestone chart was prepared. A comparison of children belonging to literate, semi-literate and illiterate parent families was done at different age levels by using ANOVA. Further a qualitative analysis of the nature of parent child interaction was done, to show the influence of such interaction on language and literacy acquisition of the child.

(b) Cross-sectional Study

A group of children were studied cross-sectionally from 2 age levels, i.e. 3 years and 4 years with 75 children in each age level. Out of 75 children 25 were taken from families of illiterate parents, 25 from families of semi-illiterate parents, and 25 from families of literate parents. Short-term parent-child interactions for 20 to 25 minutes each on two different occasions were recorded. In order to study the cognitive and linguistic and educational consequences of acquiring metarepresentational words a number of tasks were administered to the children such as: (1) appearance reality task, (2) belief desires ascription task, (3) see-know task (measuring origin of knowledge), (4) metalinguistic awareness task, and (5) task assessing emergent reading skills.

Tasks

In the longitudinal study only the frequencies of occurrence of different categories of mental state word were calculated. No other formal tasks were administered.

In the cross-sectional study two different procedures were used to collect data. First, short-term parent-child interaction for 20-25 minutes on two different occasions were recorded. Then the frequencies of occurrence of different categories of mental state word were calculated. Second, all the children were administered a set of tasks for assessing: (1) development of metarepresentation such as: Appearance-Reality task, See-Know task and False-Belief task; (2) development of emergent reading skills such as: print-awareness, pretend reading, story comprehension, word recognition, alphabet recognition and narration task; (3) development of metalinguistic ability such as: phonological oddity, semantic task, syntactic task and pragmatic task. These tasks are described in detail below:

1. Theory of Mind Tasks

Children's developing awareness of others mental states was assessed by 3 sub-tasks. The tasks are discussed briefly below:

Appearance-Reality Task

In this task children's understanding of the distinction between mind and the reality is assessed by asking them to judge what on object appears to be and what it really is? An example item is as follows: The child was presented a rope, which is painted like a snake. The child was asked to handle the rope and is convinced that "it looks like a snake but it is really a rope". Then the child was asked. "If we will ask your friend who has not touched the rope what would he say it is? "He will say it is a rope or will he say it is a snake"?

See-Know Task

This task assesses children's understanding of perception as a source of knowledge or the fact that a casual relation exists between the real world and the knowledge state. A number of such tasks have been administered to the children. An example is as follows: The child would be called upon with two of his friends. The subject child and one of his friends would be shown a doll lying in a box, but the other friend was not shown the doll. Then the child was asked "who between the two of his friends know about the doll"? The correct answer is: the friend, who has seen the doll in the box, would know about the doll.

False-Belief Task

This task was administered to examine the children's understanding and awareness of other people's belief states (i.e. "he knows" or "he think"). Such task has recently been used in the west to study children's understanding of a 'theory of mind', particularly their understanding of false belief. An example task is as follows (this is presented in the form of a story enacted by dolls):

There were two containers in the kitchen, one is big and the other is small. Leena (a small doll) put some grated coconut in the big box in the kitchen and then she went to the school. In her absence her mother prepared a cake with some of the grated coconut and the rest she put in the small container. When Leena returns from school she wanted to take some snack with the grated coconut. (At this point the child was asked a number of questions).

(1) Where would Leena look for the coconut?
(2) In which container she thinks the coconut is?
(3) Why does she think it is in the small/big container?

2. Emergent Reading Skills

A set of assessment tools for emerging reading of the children during 3 to 4 years of age would be given to explore the relationship between acquisition of metarepresentational language and emergence of reading in children. This skill has 6 different sub-tasks such as print-awareness, pretend reading, story comprehension, word recognition, alphabet recognition and narration task etc.

Print Awareness

Task A

In this task there are 4 picture cards, one card contains the picture of an ambulance and the word "Ambulance" written on it. Similarly in the other 3 cards a picture of the railway station with the words "Railway Station" and the picture of police van with the words "Police Van" written on it and a picture of the school building with the word "School" written on it was presented to the child. The child is asked to identify the print "Ambulance", "Railway Station", "Police Van" and the "School" in these 4 cards. Each correct identification is scored as "1" and an incorrect identification is scored as "0".

Task B

In this task the child is presented with 3 cards and on each card a sentence is written either on the upper, middle or lower positions. The child is asked to pretend read the sentences. Here, the investigator observes and records the eye movement of the child while he is pretend reading to see whether the child is focusing on the print or on the blank space. Correct focus on the print is scored as '1' and focus on the black space as '0'.

Pretend Reading

In the task the child is given a story book and is asked to pretend as if he is reading the book. The following observations are made by the investigator : (1) when the book is given in a reverse way whether the child is trying to correct the position of the book or° not. If the child corrects the position of the book he is given a score of '1' and otherwise '0'. (2) When the child is asked to pretend read a book, where from he is starting, from the front page or the last page. Starting to read from the front page is given a score of '1' and otherwise a score of '0' was given. (3) When the child is given a sentence to read the investigator observes whether he is pretending to read from left to right direction or from right to left direction. Left to right direction is given a score of '1' and other responses a score of '0'. (4) The investigator and the child together begin to read a book and stop at a particular point. After a while the child is asked from where we will start reading again. If the child correctly identifies the point where the investigator has left the passage, then a score of '1' is given otherwise a score of '0' is given. (5) Lastly, the investigator and the child read one page together and then pause for a while, and then the investigator asks from where to start reading. If the child correctly identifies i.e. from the next page a score of '1' is given all other answers are given a score of '0'.

Story Comprehension

A story of "Monkey and Crocodile" was narrated to the child. Six comprehension questions derived from the story were asked to the child and their responses were recorded. A score of '1' was given to the correct response and of '0' to the wrong response. The total score ranged from 0-6.

Word Recognition

Four cards were presented to the child. Three words including a target word were written on each card. The child was required to identify the target word from among the other words. Correct identification of the word was given a score of '1' and wrong response a score of '0'.

Alphabet Recognition

Sixteen cards were shown to the child on which four alphabets, A, B, C, and D was written among other alphabets, among numbers and among pictures. Each category consisted of 4 cards. The child was required to identify the target alphabet on each card, correct identification was given a score of '1' and wrong response a score of '0'. Thus, the total score ranged from 0-16.

Narration

Here, the child is asked to narrate a story of his own and is recorded accordingly. A score of 4 is given when the narration is clear, coherent and comprehensive, a score of 3 when the narration is comprehensive but lack coherence, a score of 2 is given when the child's narration is incomprehensive, '1' is given if the child attempts to narrate and '0' if the child denies. Thus, the total score ranged from 0-4.

3. Metalinguistic Task

Metalinguistic ability is the ability to analyse language beyond its linguistic principles at an abstract level or to have an objective orientation to language. It has been considered as an ability to use language to think about, and talk about language. In the context of the proposed research it is believed that acquisition of metarepresentation words would facilitate children's development of metalinguistic ability because metarepresentational terms particularly metalinguistic terms as say, ask, tell, and assert etc. would enable the child to express their knowledge of language. On the basis of this assumption, administration of a series of metalinguistic task is considered relevent. Following is a brief description of different subtasks of metalinguistic ability task:

Phonological Oddity Task

The Oriya version of this test consisted of items with 3 words per item. Two of the three words in each item formed a rhyme because of their last letter similarities. The locations of the two rhyme words were randomly varied across all the 10 items, and the subject's task was to identify the two that rhymed the same. For each item the correct answer was given a score of 1 with the maximum score being 10 for the entire task. For example, in an item Rat, Mat, Hot, the child is asked to locate the two rhyming words. Correct answer, i.e. Rat and Mat is given a score of 1, otherwise zero.

Semantic Task

(a) Ability to define words: Here the subject is asked to define a particular object to his friend. The object specified here is an elephant. The child is said that his/her friend does not know what an elephant looks like, so he will have to describe it to his friend. Here a maximum score of 5 is given depending upon the appropriateness of the definition given.

(b) Symbol substitution: The test is designed to assess the child's understanding that words are used as symbols and their meaning are not intrinsic to the words as such. The names of the objects and events can be changed without changing their properties. This test consisted of 4 questions. Thus the total number of item was 4 yielding a maximum score of 4. Each question earned a score of 1, for being correctly answered. For example, the child was first shown an "aeroplane" which was later named as frog. The child was then asked (i) what will we call this ? (ii) can this fly? (iii) how will this fly? (iv) where will it fly ?

(c) Arbitrariness of language: The test is designed to determine whether the child understands that there is an arbitrary relationship between a word and its referent. There were 2 items in the test, each one consisting of 2 questions. These items consisted of the picture of a dog and cat with the following question. If everybody in the world would agree to change names and call dogs as cats and cats as dogs, what would you call this (dog picture), what sound would this animal make?, what would you call this? (cat picture), what sound would this animal make? Correct response to each question earned a score of 1.

Syntactic Task

(a) *Appropriateness of utterance.* This test consisted of 4 items, each item presented in a social interactional situation for which the subject was required to respond. The subject was given a score of 1 for each item, if his utterance (answer) was appropriate to the occasion thus yielding a maximum possible score of 4 for the entire test. For example, the child is presented with 2 sentences such as (i) "Father, I want to go to the park", (ii) "Father, can I go to the park?", and is asked which is more appropriate.

(b) *Word Analysis Task*: The test consisted of 4 words each containing another word within itself. The child was instructed to identify the hidden word from the target word for (e.g. in "cartoon" hidden word is 'car') correct response is giveń a score of 1 yielding a maximum score of 4 for the entire task.

(c) *Correctness of other's speech:* The test consisted of 4 items, each of which was a full Oriya sentence having a structural error. As each item was read out to the child he was instructed to correctly rearrange the words in the sentences. For each item the correct response gets a score of "1" and wrong response "0". The maximum possible score for the entire test was '4'.

Pragmatic Task

(a) *Judgement of message adequacy:* This task consisted of 4 picture cards depicting different activities. The child here was given 3 messages regarding each picture card, adequate, partially adequate and inadequate messages. The child was asked to match/fit the picture from within the 3 messages given to him/her. If the child matches the picture with the adequate message that it dipicts, then he/she gets a score of '2'. If he/she matches it with the partially adequate message then a score of '1' and if he/she matches it with the inadequate one he/she gets '0'. Thus, the score for each item ranges from 0-2, yielding a maximum score of 8 for the entire test.

(b) *Say-Mean task:* The purpose of this task is to assess if children understand the distinction between the text and its interpretation, i.e. 'what is said and what is meant'. For this a situation was narrated to the child. It was as follows "Ricky had two pairs of shoes, one black and one white. When Ricky goes to school he wears the black shoes and when he goes to play he puts on the white shoes. One day after coming from the school, Ricky was in a hurry, so he asked his mother to get his shoes and his mother brought him his black shoes" and then four questions were asked to the subject child. They were: (i) How many shoes did Ricky have? (ii) What did Ricky asked his mother to get? (iii) Which colour shoe did his mother get? (iv) Whose mistake was it? Correct response was given a score of '1' and wrong response a score of '0'.

Analysis and Discussion of Major Findings

As discussed earlier the present study was undertaken to investigate the acquisition of metarepresentational words among 3- to- 4 years old Oriya children. Further, the role of parent literacy on acquisition of such words and the linguistic and literacy consequence of acquiring a theory of mind was also investigated. The data was collected by a longitudinal as well as a cross-sectional approach. The results obtained by both the approaches are discussed separately in the following pages.

Analysis of Results Obtained from the Longitudinal Study

The informal conversation between mother and child which was recorded in different situations like story telling time, meal-time, play-time and were later transcribed. The frequency of occurrence of mental state words in mother's speech and child's speech was noted. The occurrence of mental state words in child's speech over 1 year period was noted to find out the development of such words among children from 2-to-3 and half years of age. Parental conversations were also analysed to obtain the frequency of occurrence of mental state words in their speech.

Summary of Findings

(1) 2 years to 3 years 6 months is a significant period for development of mental state words. Approximately 23 different types of mental state words appear in the vocabulary of the child during this period.

(2) The rate of development is rapid among children of literate than semi-literate and illiterate parents so far as the occurrence of varieties of words are concerned.

(3) Out of the four categories more number of metacognitive and metaperceptual words started to appear followed by metalinguistic and meta-affective words in all the groups.

(4) The frequency of occurrence of mental state words among parents of the 3 year olds was more than among parents of the 2 year olds. This data was obtained only among the literate parents, as the conversation data obtained from illiterate and semi-literate parents are very few.

(5) The occurrence of different types of words like mental state words, action words, concrete words, questions, causal connectives, relational words were noted.

Detail Analysis

Acquisition of Mental State Words

A significant developmental change in the acquisition of mental state words was noticed among the children during 2- to -3 years of age (Table 4.1). Within the 2 years 6 months the children belonging to literate and semi-literate parents acquire such words like see, know, say and like. Among the children belonging to illiterate parents these words are acquired within 2 years 11 months. A rapid growth in mental state vocabulary is noticed among children of literate parents between 2 years 8 months to 3 years of age. During this period children acquire such words as: sorrow, forget, understand, ask, think, lie and truth etc. However, the rate of acquisition was very slow during this age period among children belonging to semiliterate and illiterate parents. The only word that these children acquire during this period is "cry". During the period of 3 years to 3 years 5 months the children of literate parents acquire words like: fear, mind, remember, anger, happy, desire, search and worry. In contrast except "anger" the other words did not appear in the vocabulary of the children belonging to semi-literate and illiterate parents.

Table 4.1 : The age of occurrence of mental state words among children belonging to literate, semi-literate and illiterate parents

		Literacy Level of parents		
Sl. No.	*Word*	*Literate*	*Semi-literate*	*Illiterate*
1	*Dekhiba (see)*	2yr 4 month	2 yr. 5 month	2 yr. 11 month
2	*Janiba (know)*	2yr 4 month	2 yr. 5 month	2 yr. 6 month
3	*Kahiba (say)*	2 yr 4 month	2 yr. 5 month	2 yr. 11 month
4	*Bhala lagiba (like)*	2 yr 7 month	2 yr. 5 month	3 yr.
5	*Duukha (sad)*	2 yr 8 month	—	—
6	*Bhulijiba (forget)*	2 yr 8 month	—	—
7	*Kandiba (cry)*	—	2 yr. 9 month	2 yr. 11 month
8	*Bujhiba (understand)*	2 yr 10 month	—	—
9	*Pachariba (ask)*	2 yr 10 month	—	—
10	*Bhabiba (think)*	2 yr 10 month	—	—
11	*Micha (lie)*	2 yr 10 month	—	—
12	*Sata (truth)*	3 yr	—	—
13	*Kasta (pain)*	—	3 yr.	—
14	*Shuniba (hear)*	—	3 yr. 9 month	3 yr.
15	*Bhaya (fear, afraid)*	3 yr 1 month	—	—
16	*Mana (mind)*	3 yr. 1 month	—	—
17	*Mane rakhiba (remember)*	3 yr. 1 month	—	—
18	*Ragiba (anger)*	3 yr. 2 month	3 yr. 3 month	3 yr. 4 month
19	*Khusi (happy)*	3 yr. 2 month	—	—
20	*Echha (desire)*	3 yr. 2 month	—	—
21	*Khojiba (search)*	3 yr. 4 month	—	—
22	*Byasta (worry)*	3 yr. 5 month	—	—

Frequency of Occurrence of Mental State Words among Literate Parents

As the data obtained from illiterate and semi-literate parents are not sufficient, the data from literate parents were only analysed. The frequencies of mental state words uttered by the parents are given in Tables 4.2, 4.3 and 4.4. The frequencies are more among parents of 3 years old children than among parents of 2 years old children. It suggests that parents discourse changes in both quality and quantity as the child develops in age. Parents are sensitive to the developmental level of the child.

Table 4.2 : Frequency of occurrence of mental state words among literate parents (N = 10)

Parent of/ Child's age	*Total number of mental state words*	*Mean Number of mental state words*
2 years old	77	7.7
3 years old	119	11.9

Table 4.3 : Frequency of occurrence of Metacognitive words among the literate parents (N = 10)

Parents of/ Child's age	*Know*	*Think*	*Under-stand*	*Remember*	*Forget*	*Desire*
2 years old	8	5	5	2	2	3
3 years old	10	12	8	8	7	5

Table 4.4 : Frequency of occurrence of meta-affective words among the literate parents (N = 10)

Parents of/ Child's age	*Sad*	*Happy*	*Like*	*Anger*	*Afraid*
2 years old	4	3	3	8	7
3 years old	5	4	9	3	12

Table 4.5 : Fequency of occurrence of metaperceptual and metalinguistic words among the literate parents (N = 10)

Parent/Child Age	*See*	*Say/tell*
Parent of 2 years old	10	17
Parent of 3 years old	15	21

A Comparison of Mental State Words with other Categories of Words

The language data obtained from the three groups of children were also analysed to note down the frequency of occurrence of words other than mental states occurring in children's speech. Five other categories of words such as: action word, (e.g. eating, doing, walking etc), concrete word (e.g. cat, head etc.), questions (e.g. why, which, who etc.), causal connective (e.g. that's why, because of, so that etc), and relational words (e.g. up, down etc.) were noted. A difference in percentage of occurrence of different categories of words among children belonging to the three levels of literacy was also noted (Table 4.6). A comparison of mental state words and other words shows that: (1) action words, concrete words, and relational words occurred more frequently among children of illiterate parents than literate and semi-literate parents, and (2) mental state words occurred more frequently among children of literate parents than semi-literate and illiterate parents.

Table 4.6 : Percentage of occurrence of different categories of words among literate, semi-literate and illiterate children

Literacy Level	*Mental State Word*	*Action Word*	*Concrete Word*	*Question*	*Causal Connective*	*Relational Word*
Literate	4.83	10.96	21.05	.9	.04	1.65
Semi-literate	2.41	12.25	21.5	2.64	.1	1.86
Illiterate	3.16	20.02	27.96	1.68	.08	2.05

Note: Total Number of Words: Literate (N=10) = 8969
Semi-literate (N = 7) = 2962
Illiterate (N = 6) = 1365

Analysis of Results Obtained from the Cross-sectional Study

The sample consisted of 150 Oriya speaking children selected randomly from pre-schools and Anganwadies. In each age group,

Table 4.7 : Mean scores of theory of mind tasks for 3 and 4 years and parent literacy levels

Age Level	*Literacy Level*	*See know*			*Flase belief*				*Appearance reality*		
		SKQa	*SKQb*	*SKQ(T)*	*FKQa*	*FKQb*	*FKQc*	*FKQ(T)*	*APQa*	*APQb*	*APQ(T)*
3 Years	Literate	1.00	0.68	1.68	0.56	0.80	1.00	2.36	1.00	0.88	1.88
	Semi-Literate	0.80	0.36	1.12	0.96	1.76	0.80	1.76	0.72	0.96	1.68
	Illiterate	0.60	0.28	0.88	1.88	0.60	0.28	1.88	0.72	0.60	1.32
	Total	0.80	0.44	1.23	0.44	0.63	0.92	2.0	0.81	0.81	1.63
4 Years	Literate	1.00	0.80	1.80	0.92	0.80	1.00	2.72	1.00	0.88	1.88
	Semi-Literate	0.92	0.80	1.72	0.72	0.68	0.84	2.24	0.92	0.68	1.60
	Illiterate	0.76	0.80	1.60	0.68	0.84	0.84	2.32	0.80	0.72	1.52
	Total	0.89	0.80	1.71	0.77	0.77	0.89	2.42	0.91	0.76	1.76

three groups of children from three levels of parent literacy such as: literate, semi-literate and illiterate were selected. In each group of parent literacy there were two age groups of children such as 3 years and 4 years. In each age group there were 75 children. Thus, in each literacy level, 25 children were included. To examine the acquisition of metarepresentational terms, the parent-child conversations of these children were recorded twice, primarily during meal-time for approximately 20 minutes. After transcription of the data, an analysis of the frequency of occurrence of mental state words was noted. These children were administered a number of tasks for assessing the consequences of developing a theory of mind on children's metalinguistic and emergent reading skill. The detail analysis is given below.

Summary of Findings

(1) A significant effect of age and literacy was noted in all the measures.
(2) Development of theory of mind is significantly related to performance in emergent reading tasks.

Development of Theory of Mind

To examine the development of theory of mind, 3 different tasks namely see-know, false-belief and appearance-reality task were administered individually.

The 3 year old children compared to the 4 year old children were unable to understand and explain a person's belief that was different from their own belief measured in false-belief task. The mean scores are 2.00 and 2.42 for 3 and 4 years old children respectively (Table 4.7). Similar result was also obtained in see-know task and appearance-reality task. In see-know task the mean score for the 3 and 4-year olds are 1.23 and 1.71 respectively. In appearance-reality task, the mean score for 3- and-4 year olds are 1.63 and 1.76 respectively and literacy level of parents has a positive impact on child's acquisition of a theory of mind.

In the three tasks of metarepresentation the children of literate parents showed a better development compared to the other two groups of children: children of semiliterate and illiterate parent (Fig. 4.1).

Fig.4.1 : Performance in Theory of mind tasks by children from three levels of parent literacy

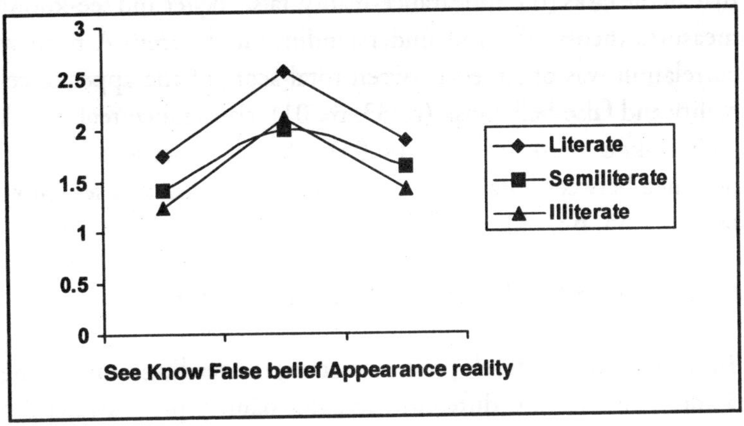

The ANOVA (Table 4.10) for see-know and false-belief tasks revealed that the children of the two different age groups and the three literacy levels differed significantly in see-know and false-belief tasks. The effect of age and literacy level were significant [F (25.00), df = 1, p<. 01 and F (9.28), df =2, p<.01] respectively on see-know task. The interaction effect was also found to be significant [F (3.65), df =2, p<. 03]. The age in interaction with different literacy levels influence the development of see-know understanding of the children. The effect of age and literacy levels were significant [F (12.64), df =1,p<. 01] and [F (7.39), df=2, p<.01] respectively on false-belief task. The interaction effect of the age and literacy level was also found to be insignificant [F (.01), df =2, p>.90]. The effect of parent literacy level was found to be significant [F (9.43), df = 2, p<. 01], where as the effect of age [F (0.21), df=2, p>. 64] and interaction of age and literacy [F (0.93), df = 2, p>. 40] was found to be insignificant on children's performance in appearance-reality task. Thus, this finding suggests that by 4 years a large number of children develop an understanding of false belief, the relationship between seeing and knowing and the distinction between appearance and reality.

A correlation obtained between the total score of the 3 different subtasks reveals a significant correlation between them, indicating that all the tasks (the appearance-reality, false -belief and see-know) measures theory of mind understanding in children. A positive correlation was obtained between total score of the appearance-reality and false-belief task ($r=.33$, $p<.01$), appearance-reality task and see-know task ($r = .21$, $p<.05$). A positive correlation was obtained between total score of the false-belief task and see-know task ($r = .35$, $p<. 01$).

Development of Emergent Reading Skills

To investigate the development of emergent reading skill among 3 and 4 year olds, 6 different measures namely print awareness, pretend reading, story comprehension, word recognition, alphabet recognition and narration task were administered individually (Table 4.8).

Table 4.8 : Mean scores for Emergent Reading Task for 3 and 4 years old children belonging to the three parent literacy levels

Age level	*Parent literacy level*	*Emergent Reading Task*						
		Print Awareness	*Pretend Reading*	*Word Recognition*	*Alphabet Recognition*	*Story Comprehension*	*Narration*	*Total*
3 Years	Literate	6.04	3.92	2.80	9.88	4.52	3.04	30.04
	Semi-literate	5.56	3.84	2.60	9.04	4.40	2.92	28.28
	Illiterate	5.68	3.80	2.44	9.16	4.40	2.80	28.44
	Total	5.76	3.85	2.61	9.36	4.44	2.92	28.92
4 Years	Literate	6.20	4.40	3.40	11.00	4.84	3.48	33.28
	Semiliterate	5.88	4.40	2.92	10.56	5.32	3.16	32.34
	Illiterate	5.44	4.40	2.88	9.88	5.28	3.28	31.16
	Total	5.84	4.40	3.07	10.48	5.15	3.31	32.23

The mean scores for all age and literacy levels on emergent

reading tasks shows that the 4 years old children showed better performance (mean=32.23) than the 3 years old children (mean=28.92) Table 4.8. The children of literate parents showed better performance or in all the subtasks of the emergent reading task than the children of semiliterate and illiterate parents (Tables 4.9). Table 4.10 shows ANOVA for emergent reading task among the different age groups and literacy levels. A significant effect of age [F (52.62), df=1,p<. 01] and literacy level [F (6.03), df=2,p<. 01] on emergent reading skill of the children was noted. It indicates that the emergent reading skills of the 4 year olds are significantly better than the 3-year olds. Similarly children of literate parents are better than the children of semiliterate and illiterate parents in emergent reading skill (Fig. 4.3). The interaction effect of age and literacy levels of parents was found to be insignificant [F(0.62), df=2, p>.54].

The correlations obtained between subtasks of the emergent reading task revealed a significant correlation between them. A positive correlation was obtained between performance in print awareness task and: pretend reading task (r=.17, p<.05), story comprehension task (r=.19, p<.05), word recognition task (r=.23, p<.01), alphabet recognition task (r=.37, p<.01) and narration task (r=.23, p<.01). Similarly, a positive correlation was obtained between pretend reading task and: alphabet recognition (r=. 33, p<. 01), story comprehension (r=. 36, p<. 01), and narration (r=. 27, p<. 01). Positive correlations were obtained between performance in word recognition and alphabet recognition story comprehension and narration task. Positive correlations were also obtained between story comprehension and narration and emergent reading total score. The relationship was positive between the score in narration task and emergent reading total score (r=. 49, p<. 01).

Development of Metalinguistic Ability

To examine the development of metalinguistic ability of the children 4 different tasks namely phonological oddity task, semantic task, syntactic task and pragmatic task were administered.

Table 4.9, shows the mean score for all age level and literacy level on metalinguistic task. The mean score of the 4 years old and 3 year olds are 39.25 and 33.91 respectively (Table 4.9). Thus, the performance in metalinguistic task was better for the 4 years old children compared to 3 years old children. So far as the mean score for metalinguistic skill for all literacy level was concerned the children of literate parent group showed better metalinguistic skills than the children of semi-literate and illiterate parent groups.

Table 4.9 : Mean scores of metalinguistic skills for 3 and 4 years old children belonging to the three parent literacy levels

Age level	*Parent literacy level*	*Metalinguistc Tasks*				
		Phonological	*Semantic*	*Syntactic*	*Pragmatic*	*Total*
3 Years	Literate	8.92	9.40	8.28	9.08	36.04
	Semi-literate	8.52	8.48	7.80	8.52	33.32
	Iliterate	8.72	8.04	7.24	8.36	32.36
	Total	8.72	8.64	7.77	8.65	33.91
4 Years	Literate	9.40	10.36	10.12	10.16	40.04
	Semi-literate	9.24	10.12	10.12	9.36	38.84
	Iliterate	8.92	10.04	10.08	9.72	38.88
	Total	9.19	10.17	10.11	9.75	39.25

Table 4.11 shows the ANOVA for metalinguistic task among the different age group and literacy level. This table revealed the highly significant differences of age and literacy level on metalinguistic skill of the children. It was found that the effect of age [F (94.06), df = 1, p<. 01] and literacy level [F (7.25), df = 2, p< .01] was significant. But the interaction effect was found to be insignificant [F(1.77), df = 2, p> .17].

A significant correlation between all the metalinguistic tasks was also indicated. A positive correlation was obtained between phonological oddity task and semantic task (r = .49, p<. 01), phonological task and pragmatic task (r = .27, p <. 01) and phonological task and total score of the metalinguistic task (r = .59, p<. 01). Similarly, a positive correlation was obtained between semantic task and syntactic task (r = .21, p <.05), semantic task and pragmatic task (r = .42, p <.01) and semantic task and total score of the metalinguistic task (r = .80, p <.01). A positive correlation was obtained between syntactic task and pragmatic task (r = .34, p <. 01), syntactic and total score of the metalinguistic task (r = .61, p <. 01) and pragmatic task and the total score of the metalinguistic task (r = .71, p <. 01).

Acquisition of Mental State Words

To compare the acquisition of mental state words in two age groups of children 4 different categories of mental state words such as: metacognitive, meta-affective, metaperceptual and metalinguistic words were identified. The mean frequency of mental state words was calculated by dividing the number of mental state words with total number of words uttered by the child on a particular occasion.

Table 4.10 : Mean frequency of occurrence of mental state words for 3 and 4 years old belonging to three-levels of parent literacy

Age level	*Parent literacy*	*Mental state words*			
		Metacognitive	*Metalinguistic*	*Metaperceptual*	*Meta-affective*
3 years	Literate	5.80	5.56	6.36	4.88
	Semi-literate	2.36	2.08	2.24	1.76
	Illiterate	2.36	1.92	2.64	2.28
	Total	3.51	3.19	3.75	2.97
4 years	Literate	8.96	8.72	9.88	8.32
	Semi-literate	6.52	5.92	7.76	5.72
	Illiterate	5.68	4.60	5.20	4.44
	Total	7.05	6.41	7.61	6.16

Table 4.10 shows the mean score for all age and literacy levels on mental state word. The 4 years old showed better performance on mental state words than the 3 years old children. Thus, the above findings suggest that as children develop, they mature cognitively and are able to use these terms effectively. Fig. 4.2 reprcsents that children of literate parent group showed better performance or high mean frequency score in all the categories of mental state word than the children of semi-literate and illiterate

parent groups. The mean-score indicates a developmental change over all the age and literacy levels. Thus, the overall result shows that the acquisition of mental state words develops over the 3 and 4 years age groups and literacy levels.

Fig. 4.2 : Development of mental state words by children from three levels of parent literacy

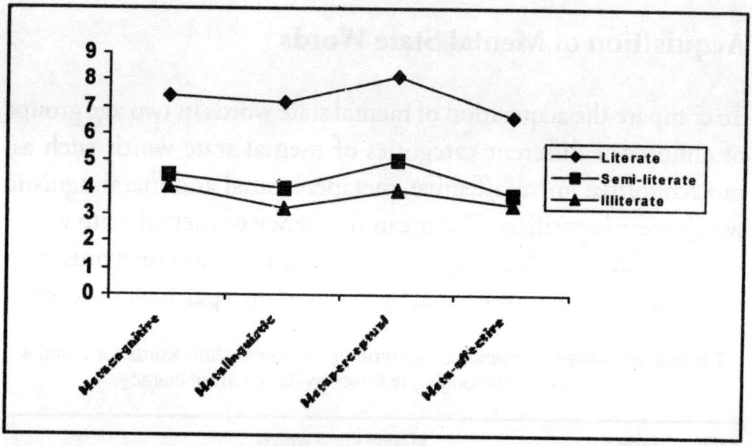

Fig. 4.3 : Performance in emergent reading task and metalinguistic task by children from three levels of parent literacy

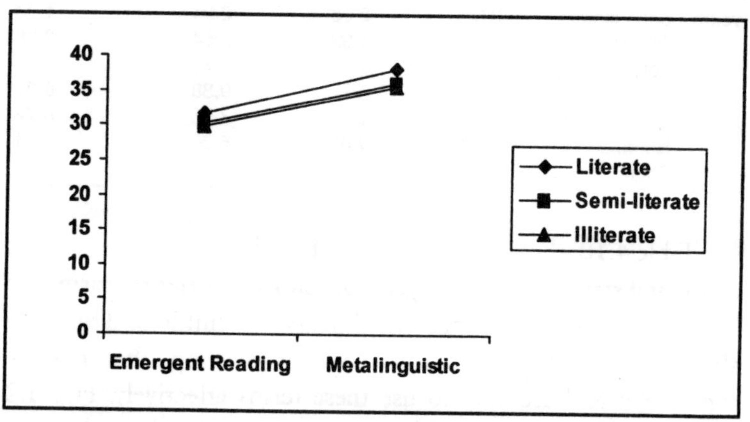

A significant correlation was obtained between children's use of cognitive and affective words (r=.77, p<.01), between cognitive

and linguistic words (r=.89, p<.01), between cognitive and perceptual words (r=.82, p<.01), between children's use of affective and linguistic words (r=.83, p<.01) and between affective and perceptual words (r=.80, p<.01). A positive relationship was also noted between the linguistic and perceptual words (r=. 86, p<. 01).

Table 4.11 : F value showing the effect of Age and parent literacy on various Metarepresentation, Metalinguistic and Emergent Reading Measures

Task	*Age*	*Literacy level*	*AxL*
See Know	25.00**	9.28**	3.65
False-Belief	12.64**	7.39**	0.10
Appearance Reality	0.21	9.43**	0.93
Emergent Reading Skill	52.67**	6.03**	0.62
Narration	14.06**	2.02	0.52

**p < .001
* p < .05

Relationship Between Acquisition of Mental State Words and Children's Performance in Cognitive and Linguistic Measures

To examine the relationship between children's acquisition of metarepresentational words and the development of a theory of mind, the frequency of occurrence of different mental state words were correlated with scores obtained from the 3 different tasks measuring theory of mind. The three different tasks were: appearance-reality, false-belief and see-know tasks.

To examine the relationship between the use of mental state words like cognitive, affective, perceptual and linguistic words and children's understanding of appearance-reality distinction (the task measuring an understanding of what it appears to be and what it really is) a correlation was obtained between the scores. It was observed that children's use of cognitive words significantly correlated with the score of appearance - reality task (r=. 28, p<. 01). A positive correlation was also found between the children's use of affective (r= .23, p<. 01) and linguistic words (r=. 27, p< .01) with the total score of appearance-reality task. Similarly, a positive correlation was also obtained between the perceptual words and total score of appearance-reality task (r=.31, p<.01). Thus there is a clear indication that the appearance reality task demands a metacognitive, meta-affective, metaperceptual and metalinguistic expression, children use these terms to explicitly express their understanding of the distinction between what it appears to be and what it really is. In other words the children who were using these mental terms explicitly in their language also perform better in appearance-reality task.

A significant correlation between total score of the false-belief and children's use of cognitive word (r=. 53, p<.01), affective word (r = .31, p<.01), linguistic word (r =.41, p<.01), and perceptual word (r = .37, p<.01) was noted. It implies that Oriya speaking children use such words to explain the other persons belief that is different from their own particularly in a false-belief scenario.

Similarly, a significant correlation between the total score of the see-know task and children's use of: cognitive words (r=.46, p<.01), between see-know task and affective word (r = .44, p<.01), and perceptual word (r=.52, p<.01), and linguistic word (r = .49, p<.01) indicated children's knowledge and use of these terms and their development of see-know understanding.

A positive correlation was observed between total score of the Emergent Reading Skill and Cognitive words (r = .51, p<.01), affective words (r = .51, p<.01), linguistic words (r =.49, p<.01) and perceptual words (r = .53, p <.01). A significant positive relationship between metalinguistic task and cognitive words (r = .50, p<. 01), affective words (r = .49, p<. 01), linguistic words (r= .55, p<. 01) and perceptual words (r = .51, p<.01). There is a clear indication that acquisition of mental state words and emergent reading skills and metalinguistic ability facilitate each other. Further research would indicate the causal relationship.

Development of Metarepresentational Words during late Childhood and early Adolescence

Further elaboration of mental state language also occurs among older children and adolescent primarily as a consequence of schooling and enriched experience in social interaction. The study reported here intends to investigate the understanding of mental state words among older children and adolescents. At the same time the the cognitive, linguistic and academic implications of acquiring an elaborate set of mental set words was investigated.

Method of Study

Design

The research was carried out with 4 (age) × 2 (area of residence) factorial design. There were four age groups of children: 6 years (Grade 2), 8 years (Grade 4), 10 years (Grade 6) and 12 years (Grade 8) from rural as well as urban areas. There were 25 rural children in each of the 4 age groups and 30 urban children in each of the four age groups, with the total sample comprising of 220 children. Their understanding of mental state words was investigated by administering metarepresentational language tasks (the detail is given later). Cognitive, linguistic and educational implication was investigated by administering cognitive-linguistic tasks and achievement tasks on science, math and by taking their class examination score on science and math.

Participants

A group of children from the age group of 6 years, 8 years, 10 years, and 12 years belonging to grade 2, grade 4, grade 6, and grade 8, respectively were taken from rural as well as urban regions of Orissa. Initially 30 children from each age (grade) level were selected for data collection. However, later during analysis 5 data from the rural area were rejected due to incomplete responses. Thus, for the final analysis 25 children in each of the four age levels from the rural areas and 30 children from each of the four age groups from the urban areas were taken. The total sample, therefore, is 220 over all the age levels and rural and urban areas. Other confounding variables like mother tongue, SES and medium of instruction were controlled as far as practicable.

Task Description

All the children were administered the following tasks :

1. Mental-state Language Task

This task has 4 sub-tasks. The tasks are discussed below:

Verb-choice level - 1

Verb-choice task measures the expression of mental state by using mental-state verb such as 'think' and 'know'. In this task an incidence involving the mental-state of the character was described. The task for the subject was to choose between the verb 'know' (referring to certainty of mental-state) and 'think' (referring to uncertainty of mental state). The correct answer was given a score of '1' and wrong answer was given a score of '0'.

Verb-choice level - 2

The children were presented with some stories in which an event was described involving a character. After going through the passage the subject was asked to choose among 4 alternatives which best described the mental state of the story character. The 4 alternatives were mental state words. For example, an item in this test was the word confirm, which was presented as follows :

"Rohit was studying in his room: Suddenly the book shelf started to shake. Rohit thought "What is going on? May be it is an earthquake". At dinner time Rohit's father said: "there was an earthquake to day. Just now it came in the news". The child was then asked to choose among the following alternatives, which described Rohit's fathers' statement."

(1) Rohit's father *predicted* that there was an earthquake.
(2) Rohit's father *conceded* that there was an earthquake.
(3) Rohit's father *confirmed* that there was an earthquake.
(4) Rohit's father *denied* that there was an earthquake.

Verb-choice level - 3

This task measures the understanding of pragmatic properties of 'think and know'. In this task, the child was told that while playing a hiding game, she would have to find a chocolate in one of the two boxes. The two dolls would each make a statement, using one of the mental verbs 'know' and 'think' referring to either of the boxes. For example, one doll might say "I think it is in the yellow box" and the other "I know it is in the orange box". The child was required to choose one of the boxes without being allowed to search for the chocolates before hand. Following this the subject will be asked an explanation question, i.e., "Why has he chosen the box"? There are 4 such items. For correct response a score of '1' was given and a score of '0' was given for incorrect response. Thus the maximum score for this task was 8.

Word Description Task

This task measures the comprehension of mental state verb such as "think" and "know". There were 8 different items and in each item an incidence was described in which the main character's mental state was highlighted. The description of the incidence was followed by two questions regarding the character's mental state. Correct answer was given a score of "1" and wrong answer was given a score of "0".

Language Task

There were two sub-tasks for assessing the overall linguistic competence of the child: (1) Reading comprehension task, and (2) Text-interpretation distinction task (or say mean task).

Reading Comprehension

In this task, children had to read one passage and then asked a number of questions. In this way the two passages of the book were presented. Each correct response was scored as 1 and each incorrect response was scored as 0. The maximum score for this task was 10, 14, 14 and 14 for the grade-2, grade-4, grade-6 and grade-8 respectively.

2. Text-interpretation Distinction Task (say- mean task)

The purpose of the say-mean task was to find out children's understanding of intention (what was meant, and their subsequent recall of expression (what was said). In this task children observed the conversational exchange between two puppet characters. Here, the daughter puppet was going to the examination and she wanted to have her "new pen" which she usually carries with her during examination time. In the cupboard there were two pens, one old pen and the other new pen. The girl was in a hurry and had already come downstairs, when she noticed that she had not got the new pen, she called her mother and told "Mother bring me my pen", thinking of course, the new pen. Then her mother brought the old pen. The listeners were then asked a number of questions. Each correct response was scored as '1' and each incorrect response was scored as '0'. Maximum score was 3 in this task.

(1) "Did mother do what the daughter asked her to do"?
(2) "What did the daughter asked the mother to bring"?
(3) "Whose fault was it that the daughter got the wrong pen"?

3. Achievement Test

A criterion referenced test for assessing Science and Math achievement was constructed by Patra (1999) keeping in view Bloom's taxonomy for each age and grade level. This test was administered to all the children. Besides the achievement tests, children's examination score in science and math was also taken.

After selecting the sample all of them were administered the tests in a random order. Per day only one or two tasks were administered to avoid fatigue or boredom of the child. The responses were recorded in separate scoring sheets and later scored. The means and standard deviations were calculated and a two way ANOVA for each task was computed. Pearson correlation was also computed by taking the responses to all the tests.

Analysis and Interpretation

Summary of Findings

(1) A significant developmental change in acquisition and elaboration of different mental state words occur between 6 to 12 years of age. Around 8 years 80 per cent proficiency in mental state words is achieved by the children.
(2) Proficiency in mental state words is significantly related to one's academic performance measured by Science Ach, Math Ach, and reading comprehension.
(3) The high scorer in metalanguage task differs significantly from the low scorer in metalanguage task in science and math achievement.

Understanding of Metarepresentational Language

Understanding of metarepresentational language refers to both comprehension and production of mental state words. Language comprehension was assessed by verb-choice tasks, word description tasks and production was assessed by the verb-choice level-3 (pragmatic task).

Table 4.12 : summarises the mean score for correct comprehension score assessed by three levels of verb-choice task, and word description task. It was evident from this table and the graphs that in verb-choice task the performance of the rural sample was better than urban sample, with an exception for 10 and 12 years old urban children whose performance was better in Verb-choice task 2 compared to the rural counterpart. Similarly, in word description task the 6 and 8 year old urban children performed better than the rural children where as the 10 and 12 year old rural children performed better than urban children. The Analysis of Variance indicated a significant difference between urban and rural sample in verb choice task-1 [F=24.83, df(1.212), p< .001] where as no such difference was indicated in verb choice task-2 [F= .09, df(1.212) p>.09] and word description task [F=.09, df(1.212), p>.79]. However, a significant developmental change was noticed in verb-choice task (1) [F=3.12, df(3.212), p<.03], verb-choice task (2) [F=18.56, df(3, 212), p<.001], and word description [F=13.94, df(3, 212), p<.001] tasks. The mean-scores in verb-choice task 3 showed a significant difference over all age groups. However, the performance of rural sample was better than the urban sample. The ANOVA shows a significant difference between rural and urban sample [F=26.20, df(1, 212), p<.001], and the four age groups [F=7.74, df(3, 212), p<.001].

Thus, the overall result shows that metarepresentational language develops over the 6, 8, 10 and 12 years age group. By 8 years of age more than 80 percent correct response to all the tests were observed. Though it was expected that performance of rural sample would be inferior, particularly in language tasks because of lack of exposure to stimulating (in terms of language experience) environment in contrast to the urban sample, the result did not confirm the expectations rather in some age groups and in some tasks rural children performed better than the urban children. Probably it was because of the fact that the rural sample was taken from a village approximately 45 km. from the city of Bhubaneswar and it was not a very remote area or the rural sample was relatively more exposed to Oriya language experiences compared to the urban sample. Though the children in both urban and rural area were taken from Oriya medium schools, the impact of English language due to urbanisation is more among the urban children, switching from Oriya to English at home and outside is more among Oriya speaking children from urban culture than the children from rural culture.

Table 4.12 : Mean Scores for Metarepresentational Tasks by Age and Area of Residence

Age	*Areas*	*Verb-Choice (1)*	*Verb-Choice (2)*	*Verb-Choice (3)*	*Wrod Discr-iption*
6 years	Rural	7.76	5.20	8	7.40
	Urban	5.77	3.07	5.87	9.80
	Combined	6.67	4.04	6.84	8.71
8 years	Rural	6.16	4.84	8	9.80
	Urban	5.57	4.43	7.47	11.37
	Combined	5.84	4.65	7.71	10.29
10 years	Rural	6.40	5.16	7.32	12
	Urban	5.80	6.00	6.93	9.90
	Combined	6.07	5.62	7.11	10.85
12 years	Rural	7.24	6.08	7.84	13.60
	Urban	5.83	6.30	7.73	10.47
	Combined	6.47	6.20	7.78	11.89

Table 4.13 : F values showing the effect of Area of Residence and Grade on various language, Achievements and Metalanguage Measures

Task	*Area*	*Grade*	*A X G*
Math-Achievement	1.6	5.45**	3.2*
Science-Achievement	3.24	9.81**	3.28*
Class Math	5.54*	24.9**	16.51**
Class Science	4.88*	11.06**	8.73**
Reading Comprehension	4.26*	11.32**	3.48*
Say mean	.04	25.21**	5.56**
Verb-Choice-1	24.83**	3.14*	2.18
Verb-Choice-2	2.98	18.56**	8.92**
Verb-Choice-3	26.2**	7.74**	8.75**
Word description	.09	3.94**	14.24**

** p < .001

* p < .05

Performance in Language Tasks

Overall language competence of the children was assessed by the language tasks. Table 4.14 shows the mean value of the four groups of children on the reading comprehension and say-mean task. It was evident from this table that in reading comprehension and say-mean tasks the performance of the rural sample was better than urban sample. In Reading comprehension task except the 10-year old the rest of the rural children performed better than the urban children. Similarly, except the 6-year-old rural children the rest of the children performed better than the urban children in say-mean task. The mean-score for the combined sample shows a significant developmental change over all the age levels (Table 4.14). A significant difference between urban and rural sample [F=4.26, df (1,212) p<.04] for reading comprehension task was observed where as no such difference between urban and rural sample was observed in say-mean task [F=.04, df(1, 212, p<0.85]. A significant developmental change was noticed in reading comprehension [F=11.32, df(3, 212, p<.001], and say-mean [F=25.21, df(3, 212, p<.001] tasks over all age groups. Interaction effect (area X grade) in both of the tasks also found to be significant.

Table 4.14 : Mean scores for Reading Comprehension and say-mean tasks by Age and Area of Residence

Age	*Areas*	*Reading Comprehension (GR)*	*Text-Interpretation Distinction Task (say-mean task)*
6 years	Rural	8.92	1.24
	Urban	7.27	1.93
	Combineo	8.02	1.62
8 years	Rural	9.80	2.76
	Urban	9.33	2.37
	Combined	9.55	2.55
10 years	Rural	6.40	2.40
	Urban	7.37	2.23
	Combined	6.93	2.31
12 years	Rural	9.04	2.88
	Urban	7.50	2.67
	Combined	8.20	2.76

Therefore, it is obvious that child's understanding of intention and their subsequent recall of expression develop over the 6, 8, 10 and 12 years age group. No systematic effect of area of residence was noted.

Performance in Achievement Tests

Table 4.15 presents the mean scores of the four groups of children for the two tests of measuring achievement. Consideration of the mean scores of the rural and urban children on the science-achievement and math-achievement tests indicated better performance of rural sample over urban sample. In science-achievement and math-achievement tests only grade-6 children from the urban area were better than grade-6 children of rural area. The mean score of the combined sample showed a significant developmental change over all the age levels. It was observed from the mean score for the class examination (science and math) tests that the grade-2 (6 year old) and grade- 4(8 year old) children from rural area showed better performance than from urban area children. Where as, grade-6 (10 year old) and grade-8 (12 year old) children from rural sample showed poor performance. In other words, only grade-6 and grade-8 children from urban area showed better results in both of the class examination tests.

Table 4.15 : Mean scores for science and math achievement test and classroom examination score for science and math by age and area of residence

Age	*Areas*	*ASC*	*AMATH*	*CSC*	*CMATH*
6 years	Rural	61.6	55.8	61.2	39.48
	Urban	47.33	43.67	56.4	46.80
	Combined	53.8	49.18	58.58	43.47
8 years	Rural	77.8	69.6	45.20	46.52
	Urban	67.33	59.5	33.37	24.93
	Combined	72.08	64.09	38.75	34.75
10 years	Rural	55.4	58.72	44.48	45.40
	Urban	62.87	70.23	66.37	60.70
	Combined	59.47	64.99	56.42	53.75
12 years	Rural	69.64	60.84	50.16	51.88
	Urban	67.7	56.40	65.73	72.70
	Combined	68.58	58.41	58.65	63.24

Analysis of variance (Table 4.13) for math-achievement [F=1.60, df(1,212), p<.21] and science-achievement [F=3.24, df(1, 212, p<.07] tests showed an insignificant difference between urban and rural sample. A significant developmental change was noticed in math-achievement (F=5.45, df(3, 212, p<.001) and science-achievement (F=9.81, df(3, 212, p<.001) tests over all age groups. Interaction effect in both the tests was also found to be significant.

A significant difference between urban sample and rural sample in class math [F=5.54, df(1,212), p<0.02] and class science [F=4.88, df(1,212), p<0.02] was indicated. This shows that the ANOVA for class math [F=5.54, df(1,212), p<0.02] and class science [F=4.88, df(1,212), p<0.02] had significant difference between urban and rural sample. Over all age groups in class math [F=24.9, df(3,212), p<.001] and science [F=11.06, df(3,212), p<.001] tests was also indicated a significant difference. The interaction effect in both the tasks was also found to be significant [F=16.51, df(3,212), p<.001] for class math and [F=8.73, df(3,212), p<.001] for class science tests. Thus, the overall result showed that achievement test performance increased over the 6, 8, 10 and 12 years age group.

Relationship between Understanding of Mental-state Language and Children's Language Performance and Educational Achievement

The verb-choice task (1) is not significantly related to any of the achievement tasks. However, it is significantly related to reading comprehension (r = .32) and word description (r = .47) tasks. Performance in verb-choice, (2) is significantly related to all the tasks except reading comprehension (Table 4.16) .The correlation is r = .46, .31, .32, .51, .23, .26, .26 for science examination, math examination, math achievement, science achievement, say-mean distinction, word description and verb-choice-3 tasks respectively. Children's performance in verb-choice-3, the pragmatic task, was not significantly related to math achievement test and math and science examination score. However, it is significantly related to reading (r = .29) and science achievement test (r = .29). Thus, the result to some extent supports the fact that one's proficiency in

Table 4.16 : Correlation between children's performance in the achievement tests, language and reading comprehension tasks

	Science Exam.	Math Exam.	Math Acht.	Science Acht.	Reading Compn.	Say-mean	Word Desn.	Verb-Choice-3	Verb-Choice-2	Verb-Choice-1
Science Exam.	1.00									
Math Exam.	.75**	1.00								
Math Achievement	.49**	.39**	1.00							
Science Achievement	.64**	.41**	.46**	1.00						
Reading Compn.	.06	.07	.19*	.18	1.00					
Say-mean	.27**	.21*	.16	.45**	.18	1.00				
Word Description	.20	.20*	.25**	.44**	.28**	.48**	1.00			
Verb-Choice-3	.16	.08	.16	.29**	.29**	.28**	.34**	1.00		
Verb-Choice-2	.46**	.31**	.32**	.51**	.11	.23*	.26**	.26**	1.00	
Verb-Choice-1	.07	.11	.16	.13	.32**	.17	.47**	.46**	.23	1.00

** .01 - .25

* .05 - .19

mental state language can influence one's academic performance particularly in science and math.

Over all language performance particularly one's reading skill assessed by reading comprehensions and text-interpretation distinction was also related to one's proficiency in mental state language. Say-mean was significantly related to verb-choice 2 (r = .23), verb choice 3 (r = .28) and word description (r = .48). Reading comprehension was significantly related to word description (r = .28) and verb choice 3 (r = .29). Thus, it can be concluded from this study that one's proficiency in mental state language is related to one's reading proficiency.

As the children's performance in verb-choice 2 the task assessing metalanguage was strongly related to children's achievement in science and math, a median split was done on scores in the verb-choice 2 task and the group was divided into high and low scores in metalanguage in the three grade levels. Subsequently, a t-test was conducted to find out the significance of difference in performance between the high and low scores in metalanguage in their respective achievement tests. Table 4.17 shows the 't' values. It was evident from this table that in grade-2 (6 years old) children's performance in science achievement, math achievement, class exam score in science and math differs significantly between high and low scorer in metalanguage (verb-choice-2). In grade-4 children's performance in science achievement and class exam score differs significantly between high and low scorer children in metalanguage (verb-choice-2). In grade-6 children's performance in science achievement test differs significantly between high and low scorer in metalanguage. No such significant difference was observed in grade-8. Though the overall result shows a trend where we can expect a significant relationship between acquisition of metarepresentational language and children's academic and linguistic performance, without further verification nothing can be conclusively suggested, and generalised.

Table 4.17 : Values showing the significance of difference between children scoring high and low in meta-language in the various achievement tasks

Achievement Task	*Grade-2*	*Grade-4*	*Grade-6*	*Grade-8*
Class-Math	3.2**	.41	1.22	1.16
Class-Science	5.06**	2.55*	1.37	.96
Math	2.92**	.92	.44	1.96
Science	2.89**	3.8**	2.78**	.6

** p < .01
 * p < .05

Chapter-5

CONCLUSION

The relationship between thought and language is a complex one. Thus, disentangling the interdependence or relationship between of theory of mind, on one hand and mental state language on the other, is not an easy task. Different psychologists have thrown light on this issue. The basic tenet of Stern's thesis of "discovery" is that ontogenetically, thought and speech develop along separate lines and that at a certain point, these lines meet. According to Vygotsky, thought development is determined by language, i.e. by the linguistic tools of thought and by the sociocultural experience of the child. Essentially, the development of logic in the child, as Piaget's studies have shown, is a direct function of his socialized speech. The child's intellectual growth is contigent on his mastering the social means of thought, i.e. language. Obviously, mastery of mental state language comes under the scope of language mastery in general. It is required for proper adaptation in social interaction and to permit reference to other's mental states. For understanding other's mental states, linguistic tools to refer to them have also to be understood.

Astington and Olson (1986) have taken the help of a Whorfian view in explaining the importance of metarepresentational language understanding. "Eskimos have many words for different types of snow and, English people have many words for mist and fog, but we do not. It is not that only Eskimos can perceive the difference between different kinds of snow and talk about them, or that only English people can perceive the difference between different kinds of fog and talk about them; others can but circuitously".

Facilitation of communication is only one of the many advantages of mastery of metalanguage. Torrance and Olson (1985) found that one of the best predictors of early reading was children's use of such metacognitive verbs as think, know, decide and remember, in their conversational interaction with peers.

As already discussed, understanding of others' mental states and one's own remains essential for every individual, where everyone acts on the basis of their construed and interpreted world, even if reality is something else. Sharing others' happiness, their sorrow, fulfilling others' desires, understanding others' perspectives, all remain at the core of human interaction. Children begin with a partial understanding of these, but very soon catch up in their preschool period itself. Further elaboration of such understanding occurs at a later age.

The research reported here was conducted under 3 major phases. In the initial phase analysis of Oriya language showed that Oriya language is rich with a number of metarepresentational words. However, the use of such words is very limited among the native speakers. Difference in use of such words was noted among different groups varying in literacy and schooling. The second phase of the research showed the development of such vocabulary during 2 to 4 years of age. Difference in development was also noted among children at different levels of parent literacy. A significant relationship between acquisition of metarepresentational words and children's performance in various cognitive tasks was noted. The third phase shows the relationship between knowledge of mental state language and children's performance in cognitive and academic tasks. Thus it can be concluded that knowledge of metarepresentational language plays a significant role on child's cognitive and academic performance.

Educational Implication

In developing a theory of mind, children begin with a partial understanding of representation. The three year olds understand mental states of their own and others. But it is not until 4 years they achieve the understanding that different people can have different perspectives of the same thing. Others may not acknowledge what one knows as reality. This strikingly matches to what Piaget called egocentrism. According to Piaget, two marked limitations of thought in the preconceptual period are found in animistic and egocentric thinking and this period is between 2 to 4 years. The child has difficulty seeing any point of view but his own. He has difficulty in seeing things from the perspective of others. The early exposure to metarepresentational concepts as well as metarepresentational language of the preschool children would go in a long way in making them more realistic, socio-centric and adaptive.

It follows from the above discussion that there is need for change from traditional to progressive philosophy of education. On the traditional side, learning is absorbing while on the progressive side, learning is constructing (Astington, 1993). This does not mean that in traditional systems, children are passive, that they donot need to think. They do think, they think about the world, they think about the task. But they do not need to think about their thinking.

In progressive systems, children are seen as constructing their own knowledge. They need to understand what it is to know and how one comes to know. They do need to think about thinking. Autistic children do not think about minds and they fare better under structured systems that do not require them to think about minds. This is not true for normal children.

Normally, by age of five years, children have beliefs about beliefs, they can attribute beliefs and other mental states to themselves and others. In the progressive setting teachers acknowledge this and encourage children to make their understanding explicit by talking about it. Even kindergarten children can be asked such questions as "Do you really know that or are you just guessing? "Did you just think of that or did you remember it?" By consciously introducing and using language about thinking in the classroom, teachers lead children to reflect on and to articulate their thinking and its expression. It may be that, by explicit ascribing a variety of mental states to children, the children will come to see themselves as holding these states.

Bibliography

Abbeduto, L., & Rosenberg, S. (1985). Children's knowledge of the presuppositions of 'know' and other cognitive verbs. *Journal of Child Language, 12,* 621-641.

Abidin, R.R. (Ed.)(1980). *Parent education and intervention hand book.* Springfield, Illinois : Charles Thomas.

Appleton, M., & Reddy,V. (1996). Teaching three year-olds to pass false belief tests: A conversational approach. *Social Development,* 5, 275-291.

Arnold, E.L. (Ed.)(1978). *Helping parents help their children.* New York: Bruner/Mazel.

Astington, J.W. (1993). *The child's discovery of mind.* Cambridge, Mass: Harvard University Press.

Astington, J.W. (1996). What is theoretical about a child's theory of mind? A Vygotskian perspective. In P. Curruthers & P. Smith (Eds), *Theories of theories of mind* (pp.1984-1999). Cambridge, UK: Cambridge University Press.

Astington, J.W. & Baird, J.A. (Eds). (2005). *Why language matters for a theory of mind* (pp.3-25). New York: Oxford University Press.

Astington, J.W. & Jenkins, J.M. (1995). *Language and Theory of Mind : A Theoritical Review and A Longitudinal Study.* Paper presented at the Biennial Meeting of the Society for Research in Child Development, Indianapolis, IN.

Astington, J.W. & Olson, D.R. (1986). *Metarepresentational language in the School : Thought and Talk about thought and talk.* OISE, University of Toronto, Ontario, Canada.

Austin, J.L. (1962). *How to Do Things with Words* (Cambridge, Mass : Harvard University Press).

Avis, J. & P.L. Harris. (1991). Belief desire, reasoning among Baka children : Evidence for a universal conception of mind. *Child Development, 62(3)*, 460-467.

Babu, N. (1989). *Children's understanding of validity and truth of mental representations.* Unpublished doctoral dissertation, University of Toronto, Ontario.

Babu, N. (1996). *Children's understanding of inference as a source of representation: A report on Canadian and Indian children.* Unpublished manuscript, Utkal University.

Babu, N., & Mamata, G. (1992). *Literacy and Mental State Understanding : A comparison of Oriya Literate, Illiterate and Oral Literate Adults.* Unpublished manuscript. CAS in Psychology, Utkal University.

Babu, N. & Mishra, S. (2000). Development of mental state verbs among Oriya speaking children: Pragmatic or semantics. *Psychological Studies, 45.* 24-29.

Babu, N. & Mohanty, A.K. (2001). Language, theory of mind and cultural construction of knowledge: a review. *Indian Psychological Abstract and Reviews, 8,* 1-47.

Babu, N. & Rath, J. (2002*) Theory of mind, culture and children's understanding of emotions.* Paper presented in the Annual Conference of National Academy of Psychology. Bhubaneswar, Orissa.

Baron-Cohen, S. (1995). *Mindblindness,* Cambridge: MIT Press.

Bartsch, K. & Wellman, H.M. (1995). *Children's talk about the mind.* New York: Oxford University Press.

Beeghly, M., Bretherton, I. & Mervis, C. (1986). Mothers internal state language to toddlers. *British Journal of Developmental Psychology, 4,* 247-261.

Berger, E.H. (1981). *Parents as Partners in Education : The School and Home Working Together.* (St. Louis, Missouri : C.V. Mosby).

Berko-Gleasen, J. (1973). *Code switching in children's language. Cognitive Development and the Acquisition of the Language.* New York: Academic Press.

Blackstone, T. (1979). Parental Involvement in Education. *Educational Policy Bulletin, 7,* 81-89.

Brentano, F. (1960). The distinction between mental and physical phenomena. In R.M. Chishalm (Eds). *Realism and the background of phenomenology* (pp. 39-61).

Bretherton, I. & Beeghly, M. (1982). Talking about Internal states: The acquisition of an explicit theory of mind. *Developmental Psychology, 18,* 906-921.

Bretherton, I.M. New, S. & Beeghly-Smith, M. (1981). Early person knowledge as expressed in gestural and verbal communication: when do infants acquire a "Theory of Mind"? In M. Lamb & L.Sherrod (Eds.), *Infant Social Cognition* (pp. 333-373). Hillsdale, NJ : Erlbaum.

Brown, J.R. & Dunn, J. (1991). You can cry mum: The Social and developmental implications of talk about internal States. *British Journal of Developmental Psychology, 9,* 297-256.

Brownwell, C.A. & Carriger, M.S. (1991). Collaborating among toddler peers: Individual contribution to social contexts. In L.R. Resnick, J.M. Levine & S.D. Teasley (Eds), *Socially shared cognition* (pp. 365-383), Wasington DC: American Psychological Association.

Bruner, J. (1975) The ontogenesis of speech acts. *Journal of Child Language, 2,* 1-19.

Bruner, J. (1978) The role of dialogue in language acquisition. In A. Sinclair, R.J. Jarvella, & W.J.M. Levelt (Eds), *The child's conception of language*, New York: Springer-Verlag.

Bruner, J. (1983). *Child's talk: Learning to use language.* Oxford: Oxford University Press.

Bruner, J. (1989). *The state of developmental psychology.* Invited address presented at the biennial meeting of the Society for research in Child Development Kansas City, MO, April.

Bruner, J. (1990). *Acts of meaning.* Cambridge, MA : Harvard University Press.

Call, J. & Tomasello, M. (1999). A nonverbal falsebelief task: the performance of children and great apes. *Child Development, 70,* 381-395.

Carey, S. (1985). *Conceptual change in childhood.* Cambridge, MA: Bradford/MIT Press.

Carey, S. (1988). Conceptual difference between children and adults. *Mind and Language, 3,* 167-183.

Chandler, M.J, Fritz, A.S. & Hala, S.M. (1989). Small scale deceit: Deception as a marker of 2-, 3- and 4-year olds early theories of mind. *Child Development. 60,* 1263-1277.

Clements, W.A., Rustin, C., & McCallum, S. (2000). Promoting the transition from implicit to explicit understanding: a training study of false-belief. *Developmental Science, 3,* 88-92.

Cutting, A. & Dunn, J. (1999). Theory of mind, emotion understanding, language and family background. *Child Development, 70,* 853-865.

Das, S. & Babu, N. (2004). Children's acquisition of a theory of mind: The role of presence vs absence of sibling. *Psychological Studies, 49 (1),* 36-44.

De Gelder, B. (1987). On not having a theory of mind. *Cognition, 27,* 285-290.

Dennett, D.C. (1987). *The Intentional Stance.* Cambridge, MA: Bradford/MIT Press.

de Villiers, J.G. (1995, March). *Steps in the mastery of Sentence Complements.* Paper presented at the Biennial Meeting of the Society for Research in Child Development, Indianapolis, IN.

de Villiers, J.G., & de Villiers, P.A. (2000). Linguistic determinism and the understanding of false beliefs. In P. Mitchell & K. J. Riggs (Eds), *Children's reasoning and the mind* (pp. 191-228). Hove, UK: Psychology Press.

Downing, J. & Leong, C.K. (1982). *Psychology of reading.* Toronto: Macmillan.

Dunn, J. (1988). *The Beginings of Social Understanding.* Cambridge, Mass : Harvard University Press.

Dunn, J. (1996). Family conversations and the development of social understanding. In B. Bernstein and J. Brannen (Eds), *Children's research and policy: Essay for Barbara Tizard.* Wasington: Taylor and Francis, pp. 81-95.

Dunn, J., Bretherton, I. & Munn, P. (1987). "Conversations about feeling states between mothers and their young children". *Developmental Psychology, 23,* 132-139.

Dunn, J., Brown, J. & Beardsall, L. (1991). Family Talk about feeling states and children's later understanding of others emotions. *Developmental Psychology, 27,* 448-455.

Farrar, M.J. & Maag, L. (2002). Early language development and the emergence of a theory of mind. *First Language, 22,* 197-213.

Fine, M.J. (ed.)(1980). *Handbook on parent education* (New York: Academic Press).

Fischer, K.W. & Bullock, D. (1984). Cognitive development in middle childhood: Conclusions and new directions in W.A. Collins and K. Heller (Eds.). *The elementary school years: Understanding development during middle childhood.* Washington D.C.: National Academic Press.

Flavell, J. (1979). *Metacognition and cognitivem Monitoring.* Unpublished paper.

Flavell, J. (1988). The development of children's knowledge about the mind: From cognitive connections to mental representations. In J.W. Astington, P. L. Harris & D.R. Olson (Eds), *Developing theories of mind,* pp. 244-267. New York: Cambridge University Press.

Fodor, J. (1992). A theory of the child's theory of mind. *Cognition, 44,* 283-296.

Furrow, D., Moore, C. Davidge, J., & Chiasson, L. (1992). Mental terms in mother's and children's speech: Similarities and relationships. *Journal of Child Language, 19,* 617-631. Printed in Great Britain.

Freeman, N.H., Lewis, C. & Doherry, M. J. (1991) Preschoolers grasp of a desire for knowledge in false-belief prediction: practical intelligence and verbal report. *British Journal of Developmental Psychology, 9,* 139-158.

Gardner, H. (1984). The development of competence in culturally defined domains: A preliminary framework. In R.A. Shweder & R.A. Le Vine (Eds), Culture theory: Essays on mind, self, and emotion. Cambridge, M.A.: Cambridge University Press.

Gearhart, M., & Hall, W.S. (1979). *Internal state words: Cultural and situational variation in vocabulary usage* (Tech. Report

No.115). Urbana: University of Illinois, Center for the Study of Reading.

Gearhart, M. & Hall, W.S. (1983). Cultural and situational variation in vocabulary usage. In L.Waterhouse (Eds.), *Individual variation in language acquisition* (pp. 89-136). Hiroshima, Japan : Bunka Hyoron.

Goldman, A.I. (1989). Interpretation Psychologized. *Mind and Language, 4,* 161-185.

Gopnik, A. (1988). Conceptual and semantic development as theory change. *Mind and Language, 3,* 197-217.

Gopnik, A. and Slaughter, V. (1991). Young children's understanding of changes in their mental states. *Child Development, 62,* 98-110.

Gordon, R.M. (1986). Folk psychology as simulation. *Mind and Language, 1,* 156-171.

Gottfried, A.W. & Gottfried, A.W. (1984). Home environment and cognitive development in young children of middle socio-economic status families. In A.W. Gottfried (Eds.). *Home environment and early cognitive development : Longitudinal research.* Orlando, FL: Academic Press.

Gruencich, R., & Trabasso, T. (1979). *The story as social environment: Children's comprehension and evaluation of intentions and consequences* (Tech. Rep. No. 142). Urbana : University of Illinois, Center for the Study of Reading. (ERIC Document Reproduction Service No.ED 177-496).

Hale, C.M. & Tager-Flusberg, H. (2003). The influence of language on theory of mind: A training study. *Developmental Science, 6,* 346-359.

Hall, W.S. & Nagy, W.E. (1986). Theoretical Issues in the Investigation of words of Internal Report. In I. Gopnik & M. Gopnik (Eds.), *From models to modules.* Ablex Publishing Corporation, Norwood, New Jersey.

Hall, W.S., Nagy, W.E., & Nottenburg, G. (1981). *Situational Variation in the use of Internal State Words* (Tech. Report No. 212). Urbana : University of Illinois, Center for the Study of Reading.

Harris, P. L. (1991). The work of the imagination. In A. Whiten (Ed.), *Natural theories of mind* (pp. 283-304). Oxford, UK: Basil Blackwell.

Harris, P. L. (1996). Desires, beliefs and language. In P. Carruthers & P. K. Smith (Eds), *Theories of mind* (pp. 20-220). Cambridge University Press.

Harris, P.L. (1999) Individual differences in understanding emotions: The role of attachment status and psychological discourse. *Attachment and Human develooment. 1*, 253-269.

Harris, P.L., de Rosnay, M., & Pons, F. (2005). Language and children's understanding of mental states. *Current Directions in Psychological Science. 14,* (2) 69-73.

Hood, L. & Bloom, L. (1979). What, when, and how about why: A longitudinal study of early expression of causality. *Monographs of the Society for Research in Child Development,* Serial No. 181.

Hopman, M. & Maratsos, M.P. (1978). A developmental study of activity and negation in complex sentences. *Journal of Child Language, 5,* 293-309

Huttenlocher, J., Haight, W., Bryk, A., Seltzer, M., & Lyons, T. (1991). Early vocabulary growth: Relation to language input and gender. *Developmental Psychology. 27,* 236-248.

Hresko, W.P., Reid, D.K., & Hammill, D.D. (1981). *The test of early language development* (TELD). Austin, Tx : Pro-Ed.

Johnson, C.N. (1988). Theory of mind and the structure of conscious experience. In J. W. Astington, P.L. Harris & D.R. Olson (Eds), Developing theories of mind, pp. 47-63. New York: Cambridge University Press.

Johnson, C.N. (1991). *From anticipation to reflection : Biological cognitive and social underpinnings of children's understanding of intentionality.* Paper presented at the Biennial meeting of the society for Research in Child Development, Seattle, WA.

Johnson, C.N. & Wellman, H.M. (1980). Children's developing understanding of mental verbs : Remember, know and guess. *Child Development, 51,* 1095-02.

Johnson, C.N. (1982). Acquisition of mental verbs and the concept of mind. In S. Kuczaj (Ed.), *Language development.* Vol.I. Syntax and semantics. Hilldale, NJ: Erlbaum.

Johnson, C.N. & Maratsos, M.P. (1977). Early comprehension of mental verbs : Think and know. *Child Development, 48,* 1743-1747.

Karmiloff-Smith, A.(1988). The child is a theoretician not an inductivist. *Mind and Language, 3,* 183-197.

Kiparsky, R. & Kiparsky, C. (1970). Fact. In M. Bierwisch & K. Heidolph (Eds) *Progress in linguistics.* The Hague: Mouton.

Lamb, J. & Lamb, W.A. (1978). *Parent education and elementary counselling,* Ann Arbors, Michigan : ERTC Clearing A House on Counselling : also by Human Sciences Press, New York.

Leslie, A.M. (1994). *TOMM, TOBY and agency: Core architecture and domain specificity in cognition and culture.* New York: Cambridge University Press.

Leslie, A.M., Friedman, O. & German, T.P. (2004). Core mechanisms in 'theory of mind'. *Trends in Cognitive Sciences, 8,* 528-533.

Lille, D.L. & Forhanis, P.L. (eds)(1976). *Teaching parents to teach.* New York : Walker.

Limber, J. (1973). The genesis of complex sentences. In T.E. Moore (Eds.). *Cognitive development and the acquisition of language.* New York : Academic Press.

Lohmann, H. & Tomasello, M. (2003). The role of language in the development of false belief understanding: A training study, *Child Development, 74,* 1130-1144.

Macnamara, J., Baker, E. & Olson, C.L. (1976). Four year old's understanding of pretend, forget and know: evidence for propositional operations. *Child Development, 46,* 62-70.

McCormick, P. (1990). *Quechua children's theory of mind.* Paper presented at the sixth University of Waterloo Conference on Child Development, Waterloo, Ontario, May.

Meins, E., Fernyhough, C. (1999). Linguistic acquisition style and mentalising development: the role of maternal mind-mindedness. *Cognitive Development, 14,* 363-380.

Meins, E., Fernyhough, C.,Wainwright, R., Clark-Carter, D., Gupta, M.D., Fradley, E., & Tucker, M. (2003). Pathways to understanding mind: construct validity and predictive validity of maternal mindedness. *Child Development, 74*, 1194-1211.

Miscione, J.L., Marvin, R.S., O'Brien, R.G., & Greenberg, M.T. (1978). A developmental study of preschool children's understanding of the words know and guess. *Child Development, 49,* 1107-1113.

Mishra, S. (1994). *Acquisition of metarepresentational language : A comparison between Oriya and English medium schools.* Unpublished M.Phil thesis, Utkal University, India.

Mitchell, P. (1994). Realism and early conception of mind: A synthesis of phylogenetic and ontogenetic issues. In C. Lewis & P. Mitchell (Eds) *Children's early understanding of mind: Origins and Development.* Hillsdale: Lawrence Earlbaum Associates.

Moeller, M.P. & Schick, B. (2006). Relations between maternal input and theory of mind understanding in deaf children, *Child Development, 77 (3)*, 751-766.

Moore, C. & Davidge, J. (1989). The development of mental terms: Pragmatics or semantics ? *Journal of Child Language, 16,* 633-641.

Moore, C., Bryant, D. & Furrow, D. (1989). Mental terms and the development of certainty. *Child Development, 60,* 167-71.

Moore, C., Furrow, D., Chiasson, L. & Patriquin, M. (1994). "Developmental Relationships between Production and Comprehension of Mental Terms", *First Language,14,*1-17.

Moore, C., Harris, L. & Patriquin, M. (1993). Lexical and prosodic cues in the comprehension of relative certainty. *Journal of Child Language, 20,* 153-167.

Moore, C., Pure, K., & Furrow, D. (1990). Children's Understanding of the modal expressions of speaker certainty and uncertainty and its relation to the development of a representational theory of mind. *Child Development, 61,* 722-730.

Morrison, G.S. (1978). *Parental Involvement in the Home, School and Community.* Columbus, Ohia : Charles E. Merrill.

Nelson, K. (1996). *Language in cognitive development.* Cambridge, UK: Cambridge University Press.

Nelson, K., Plesa, D., & Henseler, S. (1998). Children's theory of mind: An experiential interpretation. *Human Development, 47,* 7-29.

Nisbett, R.E. & Ross, L. (1980). *Human Inference: Strategies and Shortcomings of Social Judgement.* Engelwood Cliffs, NJ: Prentice-Hall.

Ochs, E., & Schieffelin, B.B. (1984). Language acquisition and socialization: Three developmental stories. In R.A. Shweder & R.A. Levine (Eds), *Culture theory: Essays on mind, self, and emotion* (pp. 276-320). Cambridge: Cambridge University Press.

Olson, D.R. (1988). On the origins of beliefs and other intentional states in children. In J.W. Astington, P.L. Harris & D.R. Olson (Eds), *Developing Theories of Mind,* pp. 414-426. New York: Cambridge University Press.

Olson, D.R. & Torrance, N.G. (1983). Literacy and Cognitive Development : A Conceptual Transformation in the early school years. In S. Meadows (Ed.), *Issues in Childhood Cognitive Development.* London : Methuen.

Papert, S. (1980). *Mindstorms: Children, Computers and Powerful Ideas.* New York: Basic Books.

Patra, S. (1999). *Achievement Tasks for Science and Mathematics.* CAS in Psychology, Utkal University.

Pattnaik, B. (1997). *The relationship between children's acquisition of a theory of mind and their understanding of metarepresentational language.* Unpublished M.Phil. dissertation, Utkal University, BBSR, Orissa.

Perner, J. (1988). Developing Semantics for theories of mind : From Propositional attitudes to mental representation. In J.W. Astington, P.L. Harris & D.R. Olson (Ed.) *Developing Theories of Mind.* pp.141-172, University Press.

Peterson, C.C., & Siegal, M. (1995). Deafness, conversation and theory of mind. *Journal of Child Psychology and Psychiatry and Allied Disciplines 36*, 459-474.

Peterson, C.C. & Siegal, M. (1998). Changing focus on the representational mind: Deaf, autistic and normal children's concepts of false photos, false drawings and false belief. *British Journal of Developmental Psychology, 16*, 301-320.

Peterson, C.C., & Siegal, M. (1999). Representing inner worlds: Theory of mind in autistic, deaf and normal hearing children. *Psychological Science, 10*, 126-129.

Peterson, C.C. & Siegal, M. (2000). Insights into theory of mind from deafness and autism. *Mind and Language, 15*, 123-145.

Premack, D.J., & Woodruff, G. (1978). Does the chimpanzee have a theory of mind? *Behavioural and Brain Sciences, 1*, 515-526.

Pugh, G. & De'Ath, E. (1984). *The Needs of Parents : Practice and Policy in Parent Education.* (London : Macmillan, for National Children's Bureau).

Pugh, G. (1981). *Parents as Partners* (London : National Children's Bureau).

Pylyshyn, Z.W. (1978). When is attribution of beliefs justified? *The Behavioural and Brain Sciences, 1*, 592-593.

Reid, J.F. (1966). Learning to think about reading. *Educational Research, 9*, 56-62.

Ridgeway, D., Waters, E. & Kuczaj, S.A. (1985). "Acquisition of Emotion-descriptive Language : Receptive and Productive Vocabulary Norms for Ages 18 months to 6 years". *Developmental Psychology, 21*, 901-908.

Ruffman, T., Slade, L., & Crowe, E. (2002). The relation between children's and mothers' mental state language and theory-of-mind understanding. *Child Development, 73*, 734-751.

Satpathy, S. (1993). *Pre-school children's understanding of perception as a source of representations: The role of metarepresentational Language.* Unpublished Master's thesis, Utkal University.

Searle, J.R. (1969). *Speech Acts: An essay in the philosophy of language.* Cambridge: Cambridge University Press.

Scoville, R.P. & Gordon, A.M. (1980). Children's Understanding of fictive presuppositions : an experiment and a review. *Journal of Child Language, 7,* 381-99.

Shatz, M., Wellman, H.M. & Silber, S. (1983). The acquisition of mental verbs: a systematic investigation of the first reference to mental State. *Cognition, 14,* 301-321.

Shukla, S. (1988). *Effect of some environmental factors on individual differences in language development.* Unpublished doctoral dissertation, Utkal University, BBSR, Orissa.

Slaughter, V. (1998). Children's understanding of pictorial and mental representations. *Child Development, 69*, 321-332.

Slaughter, V. & Gopnik, A. (1996). Conceptual coherence in the child's theory of mind: Training children to understand belief, *Child Development, 67,* 2767-2788.

Smily, P. & Huttenlocher, J. (1989). Young children's acquisition of emotion concepts. In C. Saarni & P.L. Harris (Eds.), *Children's Understanding of Emotion* (pp. 27-49). Cambridge: Cambridge University Press.

Symons, D.K. (2004) Mental state discourse, theory of mind, and the internalization of self-other understanding. *Developmental Review, 24,* 159-188.

Tager-Flusberg, H. (1993). What language reveals about the understanding of minds in children with autism. In S. Baron-Cohen, H. Tager-Flusberg, & D.Cohen (Eds.), *Understanding other minds: Perspectives from autism* (pp.138-157). Oxford : Oxford University Press.

Tager-Flusberg, H. (1995). *Language and the acquisition of a theory of mind: Evidence from autism and Williams Syndrome.* Paper presented at the Biennial Meeting of the Society for Research in Child Development, Indianapolis, IN.

Tager-Flusberg, H. (1997). Language acquisition and theory of mind. In L.B. Adamson & M.A. Romski (Eds), *Communication and language acquisition: Discoveries from a typical development* (pp. 135-160). Baltimore. MD: Paul Brookes.

Taumoepeau, M. & Ruffman, T. (2006). Mother and infant talk about mental states relate to desire language and emotion understanding. *Child Development, 77* (2), 465-481.

Tomasselo, M. (1999). The cultural origins of human cognition. Cambridge, MA: Harvard University Press.

Torrance, N. & Olson, D.R. (1987). Development of metalanguage and the acquisition of literacy: A progress Report. *Interchange, 18*, 136-146.

Urmson, J.O. (1963). Parenthetical verbs. In C.E. Caton (ed.), *Philosophy and Ordinary Language.* Urbana : University of Illinois Press.

Varley, R. (1998). Aphasic language, apasic thought: An investigation of propositional thinking in a propositional apasic. In P Carruthers & J. Boucher (Eds.), *Language and thought: interdisciplinary themes* (pp.128-145). Cambridge, England: Cambridge Unuversity Press.

Vendler, Z. (1970). Say what you think. In J.L.Cowan (Ed.), *Studies in thought and language.* Tucson, Arizona : University of Arizona Press.

Vygotsky, L.S. (1967). Play and its role in the mental development of the child. *Soviet Psychology, 5*, 6-18. Reprinted in J.K. Gardner (Eds.) *Readings in developmental psychology.* Boston, MA : Little, Brown 1978.

Vygotsky, L.S. (1978). *Mind in Society*. Cambridge, MA : Harvard University Press.

Watson, A., Painter, K. & Borenstein, M. (2002). Longitudinal relations between 2- year-olds language and 4- year olds theory of mind. *Journal of Cognition and Development, 2*, 449-457.

Wellman, H.M. (1988) First steps in child's theorizing about the mind. In J.W. Astington, P.L. Harris & D.R. Olson (Eds), *Developing Theories of Mind*, pp. 64-92. New York: Cambridge University Press.

Wellman, H.M. (1991). "From Desires to Beliefs : Acquisition of a Theory of Mind", in *Natural Theories of Mind : Evolution, Development and Stimulation of Everyday Mindreading* (pp. 19-38), (ed). A. Whiten (Oxford : Basil Blackwell), p. 34.

Wellman, H.M. & Estes, D. (1987). Children's early use of mental verbs and what they mean. *Journal of Discourse Processes, 10(2)*, 141-156.

Wellman, H.M. & Johnson, C.N. (1979). Understanding mental processes : A developmental study of 'remember' and 'forget'. *Child Development, 50*, 79-88.

Wells, G. (1985). Preschool literacy-related activities and success in school. In D. Olson, N. Torrance, & A. Hildyard (Eds.), *Literacy, Language and Learning: The Nature and Consequences of Reading and Writing.* New York: Cambrige University Press.

Wimmer, H. & Perner, J. (1983). Beliefs about beliefs: Representation and constraining function of wrong beliefs in young children's understanding of deception. *Cognition, 13*, 103-128.

Zelazo, P.D. & Jacques, S. (1996). Children's rule use: Representation, reflection, and cognitive control. In R. Vasta (Ed.), *Annals of Child Development* (Vol.12, pp. 119-176). London: Jessica Kingsley.

Index